TO DEXTER, ANNA, XANDER, AND BENJI,
WHO HAPPILY WORE EVERYTHING I EVER MADE FOR THEM.

TABLE OF CONTENTS

Knit Something You Love   7
Colorwork 101: Before You Begin   9
Tips for Successful Colorwork   14
Abbreviations List   17

THE GATEWAY SKILL   19

START YOUR COLORWORK JOURNEY WITH ONE COLOR
IN EACH HAND AND ENJOY THE RIDE

Liv Mitts (with tutorial)   29

HELLO NORDIC KNITTING   33

DIVE INTO COLORWORK WITH BOLD MOTIFS FROM
NORWAY, SWEDEN, AND ICELAND

Sander Cowl (with tutorial)   35
Swedish Lovikka Mittens   47
Lars Hat   57
Magnus Pullover   63
Maja Pullover   69
Freja Hat   75

MIND THE GAP   81

LEARN TO CATCH FLOATS WITH MORE
INTRICATE NORDIC COLORWORK

Linnea Pullover (with tutorial)   83
Setesdal Cowl   91
Dagna Hat   95
Eva Jumper   101
Greta Pullover   107
Little Greta Pullover   113

NORDIC MASTERCLASS   119

PURL WITH TWO COLORS, MAKE A FANCY BRAID, AND
PREPARE FOR A LIFETIME OF COLORWORK

Stjerne Slippers (with tutorial)   121
Little Haakon Sweater   135
Olsen Slippers   143
Selbu Mittens   151
Midsommar Pillow   159
Ingrid Fingerless Mitts   169
Kristiania Sweater   173

Basic Knitting Techniques   182
Resources   188
Acknowledgments   188
About the Author   189
Index   190

KNIT SOMETHING YOU LOVE

That's my approach to knitting in four words. This is a book for people everywhere who 1) love the look of Scandinavian knitting and 2) are motivated by the idea of making something spectacular right from the start. If that describes you, we're kindred spirits. No one told me I couldn't start with a sweater, so I skipped the plain scarf stage when I learned to knit. My first project was a Nordic cardigan. Small children in Norway learn this stuff. So can we.

STEP-BY-STEP SCANDINAVIAN COLORWORK

If you're already a skilled colorwork knitter, you may have bought this book simply because you want to make some of the projects. Great! That was the goal. But if you're new to colorwork, or even new to knitting in general, this book is for you. That's because I carefully organized the projects by difficulty to provide a step-by-step primer for all the skills you need to master the art of Scandinavian colorwork. If you're just a tiny bit adventurous and get a thrill out of learning new things, this will be a really fun ride. Don't think of colorwork as leaving your comfort zone; think of it as expanding your comfort zone in a hurry with new skills and abilities. I can't wait for you to get started.

COLORWORK MASTERY IN FIVE PROJECTS

I have taught thousands of people to knit. Along the way, I've discovered how to make colorwork click. Use this book as a helpful guide. Chapter 1 will teach you to knit and purl with your right and left hands. Chapter 2 will put both hands to work on some impressive colorwork projects. Chapter 3 will introduce you to slightly more complicated colorwork and teach you to weave in the contrasting colors to create a beautiful fabric inside and out. Chapter 4 will teach you the most commonly avoided—but super important—skill: purling in colorwork. Don't be scared. You can do it. Choose a project from each chapter, and by the end of the book, you will have mastered all the basics of colorwork by making your choice of just four or five projects. After that, the world of colorwork will be yours to explore.

I hope you love making and learning with this book!

Happy knitting,

Kristin

COLORWORK 101

BEFORE YOU BEGIN

This book is written for the knitter with basic skills who is used to working with one color while holding the yarn in either the right or left hand. It contains all you need to know to start knitting with the yarn in the other hand to help you pick up colorwork quickly and fall in love with Nordic knitting. Before you start, here are some helpful hints that will make any colorwork project a success.

FOLLOWING CHARTS

While knitting on the right side, simply follow colorwork charts from right to left. Starting at the bottom right corner, knit stitch by stitch, row by row, in whichever color the chart tells you to knit, and magically, a design will appear. When you're knitting in the round, you get to see the design unfold before your eyes. For purling (on the wrong side), read colorwork charts from left to right instead.

GAUGE: THE POWER OF MATH

No one wants a sweater that doesn't fit—not even the Weasley children! If it doesn't fit, you won't wear it. And neither will anyone else. The negative reputation of hand-knit items being too big, too small, or just plain weird comes down to one simple thing: grade-school math. Getting gauge in knitting, every time, no matter what, is really just like tuning an instrument before you play. It only takes a few minutes to figure out if your tension is correct and your stitches are the

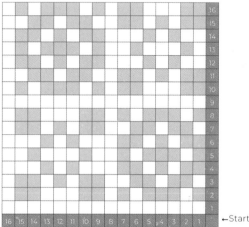

←Start Here

right size. It's a small time investment compared to all the hours it takes to knit a sweater. But it makes all the difference.

Think of it this way: You would never buy a sweater online or from a store without caring what size it is. That would be crazy. But knitting without taking time to make sure you are on gauge, and that you stay on gauge as you knit, is just that.

Getting the gauge right, and checking your gauge throughout each project, is a process that starts before you cast on and continues through the entire knit. It's not hard, but you do have to do it. When you do, your projects will turn out perfectly every time.

Have you ever heard the phrase "Measure twice and cut once"? Gauge is the measurement of knitting. Technically speaking, gauge is the number of stitches in a 4 x 4–inch (10 x 10–cm) square.

"I always get perfect gauge." If you hear this phrase, it's a lie. Every knitter knits differently. We just do. Some knit tightly and some knit loosely. And the variables that affect gauge? Holy cow! There are different methods of knitting, different types of needles, different stitches, different yarns, different ways to hold the yarn, different sizes of hands and fingers, and I'll stop there just to save space. The tiniest variance in any of these factors can make a big difference in your gauge. And, even if every one of these factors were taken out of the equation, your gauge would still be unique to you. Just like a fingerprint. That's why you have to take charge of your gauge and find the right needle size that will help you match the number of stitches to the gauge the designer recommends for every pattern you knit.

Gauge affects more than size! It also affects the weight and the drape of the fabric. If you want to get the look intended by the designer, you have to get and keep the proper gauge. Am I repeating myself? Good. It's for a reason.

I've taught many classes where every knitter in the room is making the same thing with the same yarn. With ten knitters in the class, there can be as many as five different needle sizes used to get the same gauge! In each pattern in this book, I note the needle size that I used to get the right gauge for the project. But please remember, in my patterns and everyone else's, needle size is only a suggestion. Think of it as a ballpark estimate or a starting place for swatching.

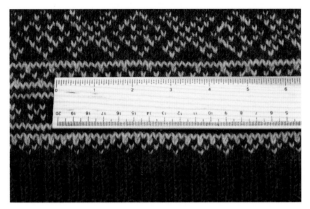

Measure a 4 x 4–inch (10 x 10–cm) area to determine gauge.

For each project, you need to swatch to determine which needle size you need to use in order to achieve the exact number of stitches per inch/cm suggested by the pattern. Here's how:

KNIT A SWATCH

1. Using the suggested needle size, knit a 4 x 4–inch (10 x 10–cm) swatch. Cast on the number of stitches for the gauge plus four stitches. The extra stitches create two selvedge stitches on each side of the gauge stitches. For example, the gauge for the Sander Cowl (page 35) is 17 stitches and 24 rows. 17 gauge stitches + 4 selvedge stitches = 21 stitches. So you will cast on 21 stitches.

2. To get an accurate gauge, you need to mimic all the methods, techniques, and materials you will be using in the project. You have to swatch with the yarn you will be using. If you are knitting in the round, your swatch has to be knit in the round. If you are knitting with metal needles, your swatch has to be made with metal needles. If you are knitting in colorwork, your swatch has to be knit in colorwork. If you are knitting with a single color, your swatch has to be knit in a single color. You get the idea.

3. If you are making a project that is mostly in a single color, start by making the swatch with one color. Before you begin the colorwork portion, do a colorwork swatch as well. Most beginning colorwork knitters knit tighter in colorwork than they do when knitting with a single color, so you may need to move up a needle size when you get to the colorwork. Swatching is the quickest way to know which size needle you need. Think of it as a shortcut.

4. If the project is all colorwork, you have to make a colorwork swatch. And if the colorwork is knit in the round, you need to knit (not purl) the swatch. The quickest way to swatch in the round is to make a speed swatch. To do so, cast on 21 stitches on circular needles, knit the first row in colorwork, then slide the stitches around the cable from the right needle to the tip of the left needle. Carry the two strands of yarn loosely behind the work to the beginning of the row and then knit the second row. You will have long strands of yarn on the back side of the swatch that connect the last stitch from the first row to the first stitch of the second row. Continue in this manner until you have knit for 4½ inches (11.5 cm). Cut the long strands at the back of the work. Trim the ends to make a tidy swatch.

5. Steam block your swatch (see page 17).

6. Measure 4 inches (10 cm) and count the stitches. (Hint: The stitches look like Vs.) If you are on gauge, you will have 17 stitches and 24 rows. Focus on the width of the stitch.

Make a speed swatch by knitting on the right side only. Cut the long strands that are carried on the back before you measure.

If you have more than 17 stitches over 4 inches (10 cm), your stitches are too small, and you need to move up one needle size and make another swatch. If you have less than 17 stitches over 4 inches (10 cm), your stitches are too big, and you need to move down one needle size and make a new swatch. Don't fret. It's only 21 stitches. Keep trying. This takes patience, but please do keep trying until you get gauge. It's worth the effort to have a garment that will fit. If you are off by just one stitch over 4 inches (10 cm), that may seem like your gauge is close enough, but when you add all of the stitches to make a sweater, that one little stitch will actually make your sweater 2 inches (5 cm) too big or too small. It's a big deal. Repeat after me. Gauge. Is. A. Thing. When you get gauge, throw yourself a little party. You are ready to cast on.

CAST ON AND KEEP WATCH

Now that you know which size needles to use, you can cast on. Keep in mind that gauge is something you need to check periodically throughout your project. As you progress, simply stop from time to time and measure and count how many stitches you have in 4 inches (10 cm). If you start knitting looser, move down a needle size. If you start knitting more tightly, move up a needle size. You can even steam block your work while it's on the needles to get an idea of what your gauge will be on your finished project.

Keeping an eye on your gauge is sort of like tasting as you cook. It tells you that you are on track and helps you avoid major disasters, like soup that is oversalted.

I check my gauge every few inches of knitting. It takes just a second. Do this, and you can rest assured that your project will turn out exactly the right size, with a lovely drape. The truth is, beautiful knits that fit perfectly don't happen by chance. They happen when you do the math. Anyone can harness this superpower to create flattering sweaters and hats that fit just right. You'll never toss a too-small (or too-big!) sweater to the back of your closet again. Gauge might be the number one thing that separates professional knitters from amateurs. And you've already learned it. Congratulations.

WORKING WITH EASE

Ease is a garment-making term that describes how tight or loosely a piece of clothing fits your body. Zero ease means skintight. Two to three inches (5 to 7.5 cm) positive ease means the garment is 2 to 3 inches (5 to 7.5 cm) larger than your actual body measurements. And so on. To find the right size sweater to knit, look at the finished bust measurement on the pattern, subtract the recommended ease (or the ease you prefer), and that number should match your exact bust measurement. Think about it this way: If a sweater is meant to fit tightly, it will have zero ease. When you subtract zero from the sweater bust size, it will be the same as your actual body measurements. It will fit like a glove.

YARN DOMINANCE

Notice how the bottom part of the swatch pictured on page 13 looks like it's gray with white and the top part of the swatch looks like it's white with gray. That's because the bottom half of this swatch was knit with the gray yarn in the left hand (the dominant position) and the white in the right hand. The top part of the swatch was knit with the white in the left hand (the dominant position) and the gray in the right.

Here's all you need to know about yarn dominance in a nutshell: When knitting two-handed colorwork (as taught in this book), you need to hold the contrasting color (pattern color) in your left hand and the main color in your right. And never switch hands. This is important and you need to remember it. So write yourself a note.

Yarn dominance is noticeable even when there is an even number of stitches of each color. On the bottom half of this swatch the gray yarn is dominant, and the fabric looks like it's gray with white squares. On the top, the white yarn is dominant and the fabric looks white with gray squares.

Yarn dominance on the flipside. From the bottom up, there are two rows of navy, then one row of white, finally one row of navy and then the colorwork begins. Notice on the first row of colorwork that the white strand runs below the navy strand. That means the white strand is in the dominant position on the right side.

That's the short version. If you want to understand why, here's the PhD version: The term "dominant yarn" can be a confusing phrase. Some knitters think "dominant yarn" or "dominant color" means the main color of the sweater (logical, but untrue). The dominant color refers to the yarn in the dominant position. In two-handed colorwork, because of tension and position, the yarn you hold in your left hand will be a bit bolder. It makes the stitch pop. A simple rule of thumb: The yarn to the left is in the dominant position. For this reason, the contrasting color (or color of the pattern) is always held in your left hand, and the main color (or color of the background) is held in your right. This puts the pattern color in the dominant position.

Have you ever seen colorwork knitting where the pattern stitches recede, and even disappear? That is a perfect example of the pattern stitches not being in the dominant position.

Note that there is a very small percentage of knitters for whom the opposite is true—the dominant position is with the yarn held to the right. So, the best thing to do is start by holding the contrasting color of yarn in your left hand. If you have a dominance problem and your colorwork looks muddy, switch the contrasting color to your right hand to see if that helps your pattern become crisp and clear. If so, then you are the exception. Know that, and make sure you always use your unique yarn-dominance position.

PRO TIP: All of the above applies to two-handed, two-color colorwork. If you are knitting with three colors, or otherwise knitting while holding two strands in one hand, the left-dominance rule still applies, and the contrasting color needs to be held to the left of the main color in your hand.

TROUBLESHOOTING: One easy way to check yarn dominance is to look at the back of your work. In stranded colorwork, two strands run parallel to each other along the wrong side of the garment. When looking at these two strands, the dominant yarn is the one situated on the bottom.

TIPS FOR SUCCESSFUL COLORWORK

1. **MEMORIZE THE PATTERN.** Don't be over-whelmed by this. I'm not asking you to memorize the whole chart, just the sequence of stitches in a single row. The patterns in this book are all fairly simple and easy to memorize line-by-line. As you gain more experience knitting in colorwork, your ability to see and memorize small sections, or repeating motifs, within the larger pattern will increase. It's super good for your brain. And every time you memorize a row within the chart, you can knit away without being tied to the chart. The freedom from having to look at the chart constantly makes knitting colorwork much more fun and enjoyable. You can always check the chart for reference if you feel unsure, but try your best to establish chart independence.

2. **USE VISUAL RELATIONSHIPS.** Look at the relationship between the stitches on your left needle (your last row knit) and the row you are about to knit. Use your knitting as a guide. Look for visual cues. Don't just count stitches. This is how I do it. I first analyze the shape.

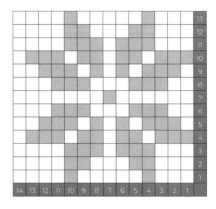

Look at the first row of this traditional Selbu Star in the chart above. On the first row of a pattern, you need to count carefully to establish the pattern. Notice how there are two legs of the star. Beginning right to left, this pattern has three white stitches, one black, five white, one black, then four white stitches.

> **NOTE:** When this chart is repeated, the last four stitches and the first three stitches run together so that you knit seven white stitches between each star.

Now look at the second row. Start to see shapes. There are two black stitches on top of the "legs" of the star. Notice the relationship of those stitches to the black stitches in the first row. See how the star is symmetrical? You can knit the first side of the star and then knit its mirror image, horizontally, practically without even thinking about it.

Look at the third row. See the three stitches on the "legs" of the star? Using the row below as your guide, you can now knit the third row, without even looking at the chart, using your knitting as a guide instead. Row 4 has the "arms" of the star, so knit those. Line upon line, you are building the image in the chart. On rows 5 and 6, notice that the "arms" of the star always have three stitches and are just one stitch to the left (or to the right) of the line below. As the "arms" of the star grow, the "legs" get smaller. Row 7 is super easy because you knit with all white stitches except for one black stitch in the center of the star. Rows 8–13 are easy, because you simply knit the top of the star, which is a mirror image of the rows you just knit below. You can use your knitting as a portable graph.

> **FUN TIP:** Sometimes it's helpful to get out some graph paper and redraw the chart by hand before you knit. Doing this gets you familiar with the pattern relationships and makes knitting easier because you already have the chart in your head.

3. **USE YOUR KNITTING AS YOUR CHART.** This is super helpful when you are knitting an overall pattern that repeats. Once the pattern is established in your knitting, you can simply use your knitting as your chart. You can easily do this with the Sander Cowl (page 35), the heel of the Olsen Slippers (page 143) and the Stjerne Slippers (page 121), the Setesdal Cowl (page 91), and the Dagna Hat (page 95). I love knitting colorwork away from charts! Try it!

4. **MARK THE ROW YOU ARE KNITTING ON THE CHART.** Some beginners like to mark their current row on the chart as they knit to keep their place. If you choose to do this, you can use highlighter tape, a sticky note, or a piece of paper. You may be tempted to cover up the rows below the row you are knitting. Don't. You may cover up the chart above the row you are working on, but never cover up the rows below. You will get lost and make mistakes if you don't have the rows below to use as a reference.

5. **USE HIGH-CONTRAST YARN COMBINATIONS.** This matters when you are new to knitting colorwork. Low-contrast colorwork can be beautiful, but be warned, it is significantly more difficult to knit. And if color values are too similar, you won't be able to see the colorwork anyway. Here's a pro tip: Take a simple phone photo of the yarn skeins you are thinking of using in your project and then make the photo black and white. If you can see a difference between the two colors in a black-and-white photo, you are good to go. If the values are too similar, the yarns will look like the same color in black and white. I always check values this way. It's a super helpful trick.

6. **BE CONSISTENT.** As mentioned earlier, always knit with the contrasting color (or pattern color) in your left hand and the main color in your right hand. Remember, yarn dominance is super important!

7. **CATCH FLOATS.** Floats are the strands of yarn on the back side of your knitting that occur when you are not knitting with one of the colors. You don't want to have long floats because they can catch on fingers or jewelry, and when you have long floats, they can inhibit the stretch of the fabric. You will want to catch the float, so the strand is incorporated into the fabric.

I would suggest that whenever you have more than five consecutive stitches of a single color in a row, you will need to catch the float of the color you are not using. See Chapter 3 (page 85) for a tutorial.

8. **WEAVE IN AND WEAVE OUT.** When adding a second color, weave in the yarn (catch the float every other stitch; see Chapter 2, page 38) for seven stitches before you start knitting with it, and when you are done with a color, weave out the tail for seven stitches as well. It doesn't take any time to weave your yarn in and out, but it will save you hours of weaving in ends when you are finished.

9. **STEAM BLOCK.** It's magic! Because some methods of blocking require a finished project—soaking, pinning to a board, etc.—knitters often think of blocking as a final step. But I prefer steam blocking. It's a terrific method that lets you block your project as you go. That way you can block your swatches, block your project on the needles, and of course, block when you're done. All you need to steam block is two tea towels, water, and an iron. Soak both cotton dishtowels and wring them out. Lay one towel out on your ironing board, place your knitting on top, and cover it with the second towel. Then press with a hot iron. The wet towels protect your knitting. The steam relaxes the fibers and immediately blocks your knitting to make the stitches even and flat. Try it! It's so nice to see your knitting blocked and flat and crisp. It's very good for your knitting self-esteem! Just remember never to block the ribbing. If you do, it will lose its shape.

10. **WORK WITH BEAUTIFUL YARN.** This may sound painfully obvious. But I often see skilled knitters spend valuable time and life energy crafting beautiful patterns with subpar yarn. And then they wonder why their projects don't look like the pattern photos. If you're going to the trouble to make a garment by hand, start with beautiful wool and make something you will love. You are spending a lot of time here. Match that valuable commodity with beautiful materials. Make an heirloom.

SKILL LEVELS

Everything in this book was designed with beginners in mind. That said, the projects here do involve cumulative skills that, by the final chapter, will prepare you to navigate the wider world of colorwork. Please don't be intimidated by projects labeled intermediate. All of the projects in *The Nordic Knitting Primer* were carefully designed to involve only a light amount of challenging skills. Just enough to learn from.

✸ **BEGINNER.** Super easy. You can make these projects even if you've never touched a knitting needle before.

✸ ✸ **ADVENTUROUS BEGINNER.** Still learning. If you can knit holding the yarn in both hands (and can purl in one hand), you can do these projects.

✸ ✸ ✸ **INTERMEDIATE 1.** More intricate patterns that require catching floats.

✸ ✸ ✸ ✸ **INTERMEDIATE 2.** Intricate patterns that require colorwork knitting with a small amount of colorwork purling.

ABBREVIATIONS LIST

BOR = beginning of round

CC = contrast color

CM = centimeter(s)

DPN = double-pointed needles

GSR = German short rows

K = knit

K2TOG = knit two stitches together; see page 184

M = meter(s)

MC = main color

P = purl

P2TOG = purl two stitches together

RS = right side

SL1 K2TOG PSSO = slip one stitch, knit the next two stitches together, then pass the slipped stitch over; see page 186

SSK = slip two stitches knitwise, then knit them together; see page 186

WS = wrong side

THE GATEWAY SKILL

START YOUR COLORWORK JOURNEY WITH ONE COLOR
IN EACH HAND AND ENJOY THE RIDE

Knitting is a folk art, passed from generation to generation, with a gazillion variations depending on when and where knitters learned to knit, who taught them, and possibly even where they were born. There are fabulous knitting traditions around the world, and there are no right and wrong ways to knit, only techniques to learn from. In Western knitting, there are primarily two ways to knit with a single color: Continental knitting (holding the yarn in the left hand) and English knitting (holding the yarn in the right hand). Logically, most colorwork methods stem from a variation of Continental or English knitting. While some knitters might switch between these methods, most settle on one that works best for them.

The colorwork methods are:

1. holding both colors of yarn in the left hand (Continental, or German knitting)

2. holding both colors of yarn in the right hand (English knitting)

3. holding one color of yarn in each hand (the best of both worlds)

Not surprisingly, a lot of Scandinavian knitters use the Continental method when knitting with two colors. But many also use the third method—a wonderfully inclusive mash-up of both knitting traditions—which I'll be teaching in this book. Here's its story:

The famed knitting author Elizabeth Zimmermann (whose PBS television show taught my generation to knit) had a nanny from the U.K. who encouraged her to hold the yarn in her right hand, and a nanny from Switzerland who always knit with the yarn in her left. To knit in colorwork, Elizabeth combined the two knitting traditions and held one color in her right hand and one in her left. Whether or not she was the first person in history to tackle colorwork this way doesn't matter. She made it popular. And it turns out she was on to something big.

Two hands. Two colors. It just makes sense.

Just because all colorwork methods work, that doesn't mean they all have the same learning curve. After teaching colorwork for half a lifetime, I have found that the two-handed method is simply the fastest and easiest way for beginners to grasp and fall in love with two-color knitting.* Whichever way you knit, when you combine the way you already know how to knit with holding the yarn in the opposite hand, something miraculous happens. I've had knitting students shout with joy in class when it clicks.

*If you're curious, I use two methods in my own colorwork knitting. I frequently knit with one color in each hand (as taught here), but sometimes I choose to knit with two colors in my left hand as well. I simply consider the latter a more advanced skill.

Your newfound ambidexterity will make your knitting better in a number of ways that come in handy when you least expect it, including:

1. Your yarn won't get tangled, so you can knit faster!

2. Your brain can easily read a colorwork chart and transfer it to your hands—left hand carries pattern color, right hand carries background color. Honestly, when I knit in colorwork, it's so automatic, I don't even think about it.

3. It's very easy to catch floats, eliminating long strands on the back side of your work and adding stretch to the finished garment. See Chapter 3, page 85.

4. Learning to knit with yarn in both hands gives you the coordination to handle even more advanced skills in the future, like knitting three colors at once.

5. Learning to knit in a new way will make both of your hands more nimble, increasing your dexterity and coordination.

6. Best of all, it will introduce you to the way other people knit. Learning to walk in other knitters' shoes, in life and in knitting, is always a good thing. And it may even change your preferred way to knit.

LET'S GET STARTED

Remember how awkward knitting was when you first began? And remember how nice it was when that awkwardness disappeared and knitting became comfortable and easy? Well, you are about to go through all of that again. But not for long. There are differences you will notice right away between knitting with the yarn in the hand you are used to and knitting with the yarn in your opposite hand. Continental knitting is also called "picking." If it's new to you, you'll notice the right needle has a bigger job to do in this method. There's more motion with the right needle to go and fetch the yarn off the left finger. Likewise, English "throwing" feels really strange to Continental knitters. You may ask yourself, "How do I get the yarn way over there?" Just know that it will feel weird to hold the yarn in a different hand for the first day or so. One knitter complained that I had *ruined* knitting for her! "It used to feel comforting," she cried, "and now it is horrible!" But soldier on, my friend. After you practice just a little, stop and sleep on it. I promise you, the next day knitting in this new way will start to feel a little more comfortable, and even natural. In a few days, it will be positively easy. That knitter I just told you about? She fell in love with holding the yarn in her opposite hand just 24 hours later. I know you will too.

Even if you don't immediately learn to love this new-to-you method of knitting right away, just wait until you bring it all together in colorwork. Once you start knitting in two colors with the simple and logical method of holding one strand in each hand, your old way of knitting and your new way will come together like magic—all the comfort of how you used to knit, combined with a new superpower.

Practice knitting with the yarn in a different hand than you are used to by making a pair of Liv Mitts (page 29). I designed this project exclusively to help knitters get used to knitting (and purling) with the yarn in their unfamiliar hand. It's all about leaving your comfort zone and trying something new. Bravely make a pair of mitts in the manner of knitting that's new to you, and I promise your effort will pay off big time! You'll get used to the new method in one weekend and pick up a skill that will make learning colorwork easy. If you are new to knitting altogether, you can make as many pairs of Liv Mitts as it takes to get comfortable with knitting and purling with the yarn in either hand.

HOW TO HOLD THE YARN IN YOUR LEFT HAND

1.

Wrap the yarn clockwise around your left pinky finger.

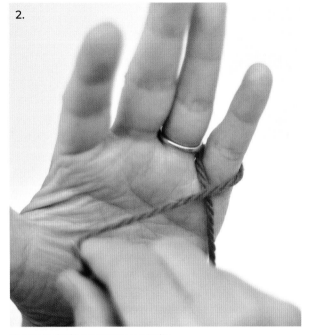

2.

Continue clockwise across your palm . . .

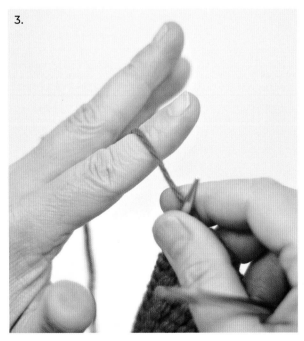

3.

. . . and counterclockwise over your index finger.

4.

Ready to knit.

HOW TO KNIT WITH THE YARN IN YOUR LEFT HAND: A POEM

1.

Prepare to enter from the left side of the first stitch on the left needle.

2.

Under the gate: Insert the right needle through the stitch.

3.

Capture the sheep: Pick the yarn off your left-hand finger.

4.

Back they come: Pull the yarn through the stitch.

5.

And off they leap: Transfer the new stitch from the left needle to the right needle.

HOW TO PURL WITH THE YARN IN YOUR LEFT HAND: A POEM

1.

Enter downward from the right side of the first stitch on the left needle; notice that the yarn is in position to go counterclockwise over the top of the right needle.

2.

Down the bunny hole: Place your thumb on top of the working yarn, and pull the yarn straight down toward the front side of the work.

3.

Around the big tree: Yarn goes over the top and counterclockwise around the needle. The left thumb helps anchor the yarn.

4.

Up pops the bunny: Pull the yarn back through the stitch with an upward motion.

5.

And off goes she: Transfer the new stitch from the left needle to the right needle.

NOTE: This is how I purl. It takes a bit of practice but makes Continental purling easy to do and in the future, when you are knitting with three colors, you will be able to easily purl with two colors in your left hand. With this method, your thumb is able to move between two strands, selecting whichever color you need.

HOW TO HOLD THE YARN IN YOUR RIGHT HAND

1.

Wrap the yarn counterclockwise around your right pinky finger.

2.

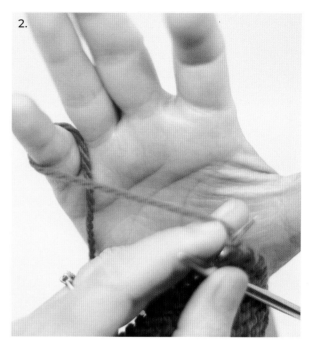

Continue counterclockwise across your palm . . .

3.

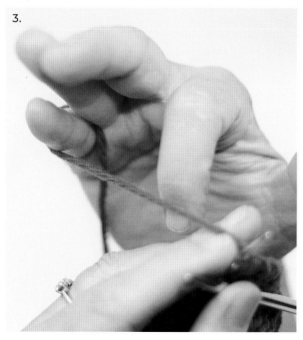

. . . and clockwise over your index finger.

4.

Ready to knit.

HOW TO KNIT WITH THE YARN IN YOUR RIGHT HAND: A POEM

1.

Prepare to enter from the left side of the first stitch on the left needle.

2.

In through the front door: Insert the right needle up through the stitch.

3.

Once around the back: Wrap the yarn from the back to the front around the needle.

4.

Peek through the window: Pull the yarn through the stitch.

5.

And off jumps Jack: Lift the new stitch from the left needle onto the right needle.

HOW TO PURL WITH THE YARN IN YOUR RIGHT HAND: A POEM

1.

Prepare to enter from the right side and downward into the first stitch on the left needle.

2.

Jack goes in: Insert the right needle into the stitch.

3.

Puts on his scarf: The yarn goes counterclockwise over the top and around the right needle.

4.

Comes out back: Pull the yarn back through the stitch with an upward motion.

5.

And takes it off: Transfer the new stitch from the left needle onto the right needle.

LIV MITTS

✳ BEGINNER

Liv Mitts are shaped with a subtle picot edge that creates a stunning and versatile wrist warmer. Knit in lovely Woolfolk Får, they feel like a little luxury every time you wear them. Why begin a book on Scandinavian colorwork with a pair of one-color garter stitch mitts? To sharpen your knitting skills in any direction you may require. Because garter stitch involves knitting (or purling) on both the right side and the wrong side of the fabric, the practice possibilities here are endless. Simply make a pair holding the yarn in your unfamiliar hand, knitting one mitt and purling the other. It's like a practice swatch that just happens to yield a beautiful pair of mitts at the end. You'll be surprised how cozy you feel when your wrists are warm.

SKILLS YOU'LL PRACTICE

Long-tail cast on (page 184). Knitting and purling with yarn in either hand (page 19). Garter stitch. K2tog decrease (page 184). Making a picot edge (page 185). Binding off (page 182). Mattress stitch (page 185).

SIZE

One size fits most

MATERIALS

YARN: Worsted | Woolfolk Får | 100% Ovis 21 Ultimate Merino | 142 yards (130 m) per 1.75-ounce (50-g) skein | 1 skein | Color: 27 (Gold)

Approximately 94 yards (86 m) per pair of mitts

NEEDLES: Pair of knitting needles, any length, in size needed to obtain gauge

SUGGESTED NEEDLE SIZE: US 4 (3.5 mm)

ADDITIONAL MATERIALS

Tapestry needle and scissors

GAUGE AND SWATCH

22 stitches and 36 rows = 4 inches (10 cm)

Worked in garter stitch

FINISHED MEASUREMENTS

7½ x 6–inch (19 x 15.25–cm) rectangle; 3¾ x 6–inch (9.5 x 15.25–cm) mitt

INSTRUCTIONS

1. CAST ON

With gauge-size needles, using a long-tail cast on, cast on 31 stitches.

2. WORK MITT WITH GARTER STITCH HOLDING THE YARN IN THE RIGHT OR THE LEFT HAND, WHICHEVER WAY IS NEW TO YOU

ROW 1: (RS) Knit 30 stitches and on Stitch 31, increase one stitch by knitting into the front and the back of the stitch. Turn. Total stitches: 32.

ROW 2: (WS) Knit 32 stitches. Turn.

ROW 3: (RS) Knit 31 stitches and on Stitch 32, increase one stitch by knitting into the front and the back of the stitch. Turn. Total stitches: 33.

ROW 4: (WS) Bind off 2 stitches. Knit 30 stitches. Turn. Total stitches: 31.

Work Rows 1–4 seventeen times (or until the mitt measures 7½ inches [19 cm]). On the last Row 4, bind off all stitches. Break the tail and leave an 18-inch (46-cm)-long tail to be used to sew the mitt together.

3. SEW THE MITT TOGETHER

With the right side facing out, join the first knit row above the cast-on row to the last knit row below the bind-off row with a mattress stitch. This method puts the seam on the inside of the mitt. See the tutorial on page 185.

4. FINISHING

Weave in the ends. Hurray! You're done! Block. Gift. Warm. Love.

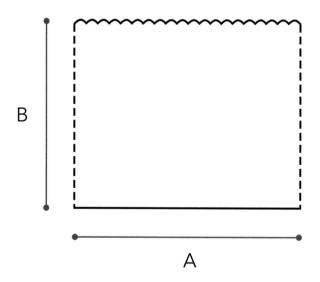

LIV MITTS SCHEMATIC

A- Width: 7½ inches (19 cm)

B- Length: 6 inches (15.25 cm)

HELLO NORDIC KNITTING

DIVE INTO COLORWORK WITH BOLD MOTIFS FROM NORWAY, SWEDEN, AND ICELAND

You can do this. At first glance, the beautiful projects in this chapter may all look too difficult for beginners. That's a happy illusion. I agree that no one will believe any of these knits were your first colorwork project. That's the fun part. I promise all of the patterns in this chapter were designed to teach beginning colorwork. I've used tricks like fat yarn (which knits up quickly), bold patterns with simple repeats, traditional and uncomplicated Nordic garment construction, and sweaters that are 60 to 75 percent plain knitting (which you can handle in whichever method you prefer).

You can learn Nordic colorwork with any pattern in this chapter, so start anywhere. My advice is to find the project you are the most excited about. Creating something you love is a powerful motivational tool. And don't be afraid to start with a sweater. Colorwork sweaters come with a very high effort-to-reward ratio. If you go there, note that the Magnus Pullover (page 63) is slightly easier than the Maja Pullover (page 69). But both are doable. If you're on the lookout for the easiest colorwork project in the book, it's the Lars Hat (page 57). The Swedish Lovikka Mittens (page 47) are a good place to practice your plain knitting because the colorwork is added with embroidery at the end. They'll also teach you to wrangle five double-pointed needles at once—a valuable skill. If you want to jump right into all-over colorwork, start with the Sander Cowl (page 35). If you are up for a challenge, check out the beautiful Freja Hat (page 75). I'm warning you, colorwork is addicting.

Wherever you begin, please read the colorwork tutorial included with the Sander Cowl pattern. It's your introduction to two-handed colorwork. Don't miss it. If you've learned to knit with the yarn in both hands, you are ready to go. Put the pattern color in your left hand, the background in your right hand, and knit something beautiful!

SANDER COWL

✹✸ ADVENTUROUS BEGINNER

In the frosty north, two-color knitting was invented to make a thicker and warmer garment. Beyond this practical side of stranded knitting, colorwork adds contrast, pattern, and beauty. Besides, colorwork is a blast to knit. This cowl looks complicated, but it is really just a simple XO pattern repeat. It's knit in the round, with minimal shaping, so you can concentrate on colorwork without worrying about anything else. In Norwegian, patterns like this one with an XO repeat are called *Kors og Kringle*, which translates to Cross and Cookie. Don't you love that? But I digress. All you have to do is follow the chart from right to left, working row by row from the bottom row to the top row of the chart. Start with Stitch 1. Put the contrasting color (black) in your left hand and the main color (white) in your right hand; knit the colors you see on the chart in order and the design will magically appear. This pattern is designed with two 7 x 7 stitch patterns. Knit a cross. Knit a cookie. Repeat.

SKILLS YOU'LL PRACTICE

Long-tail cast on (page 184). Joining in the round seamlessly (page 37). Working 2x2 ribbing (k2, p2). Weaving a new yarn color in (and out) (pages 38–39 and 44–45). Knitting with two colors in the round, left and right together (pages 41–42). Reading a chart (page 9). Backward loop increase (page 182). K2tog decrease (page 184). Binding off (page 182). Duplicate stitch join (page 183).

SIZE

One size fits most

MATERIALS

YARN: Worsted | Woolfolk Får | 100% Ovis 21 Ultimate Merino Wool | 142 yards (130 m) per 1.75-ounce (50-g) skein

MAIN COLOR (MC): 00 (White) | 2 skeins

CONTRASTING COLOR (CC): 1515 (Black) | 1 skein

NEEDLES

NEEDLES: One 24-inch (60-cm) circular needle in size needed to obtain gauge in colorwork

SUGGESTED NEEDLE SIZE: US 6 (4 mm)

One 24-inch (60-cm) circular needle one size smaller than gauge-size needles

SUGGESTED NEEDLE SIZE: US 5 (3.75 mm)

ADDITIONAL MATERIALS

Stitch marker, tapestry needle, and scissors

GAUGE AND SWATCH

23 stitches and 27 rounds = 4 inches (10 cm)

Worked in stranded colorwork in the round with larger needles

FINISHED MEASUREMENTS

12½ x 8½ inches (31.75 x 21.5 cm)

INSTRUCTIONS

1. CAST ON

With smaller needles and the MC, using a long-tail cast on, cast on 140 stitches.

2. JOIN AND WORK RIBBING

Join to knit in the round, being careful not to twist the cast-on stitches. Round 1: Place marker at the beginning of the round. *Knit 2, purl 2.* Repeat from * to * all the way around. Work 2x2 ribbing for another eight rounds. For a beautiful join, follow the photo tutorial on the opposite page.

CREATING A SEAMLESS JOIN: When you knit in the round, there can be a gap from the last stitch of the cast-on row to the first stitch of the first knit row. This can be avoided by following the tutorial for joining in the round.

3. KNIT TWO ROUNDS WITH MAIN COLOR AND INCREASE 4 STITCHES

Continuing with the MC, knit one round and increase 4 stitches evenly spaced with a backward loop in this manner: *Knit 35 stitches and make one stitch with a backward loop.* Knit from * to * four times. Total stitches: 144. Knit one round and stop 7 stitches before the marker and weave in the CC so that you are ready to begin with both colors after the marker.

JOINING IN THE ROUND

1.

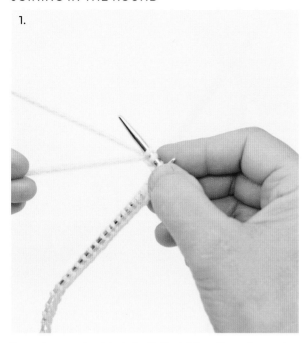

To create a seamless join, knit with the tail from the cast on and the working yarn.

2.

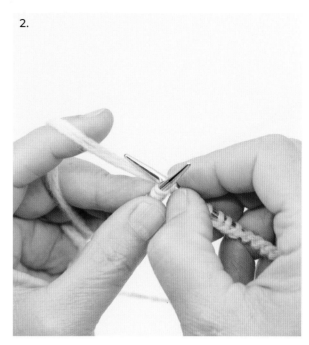

Insert the right needle into the first stitch on the left needle, while holding the tail and the working yarn together over the left index finger. Tug on the yarn a bit to pull the last cast-on stitch of the round snugly next to the first cast-on stitch of the round.

3.

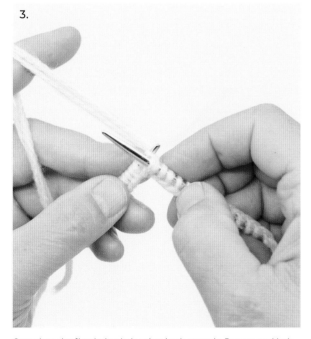

Complete the first knit stitch using both strands. Repeat and knit the second stitch, also with two strands.

4.

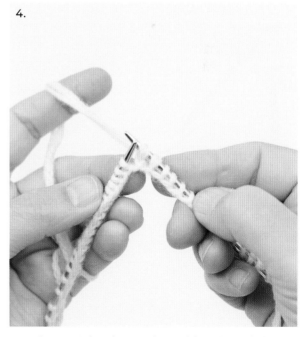

Note: The two stitches closest to the tip of the right needle have two strands. On Row 2, treat the two strands on each stitch as one.

WEAVING IN A NEW COLOR

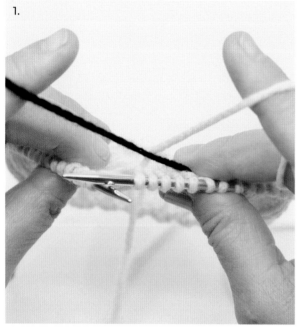

1.

Seven stitches before beginning colorwork, put the new yarn over the working yarn and hold it in place with your right middle finger.

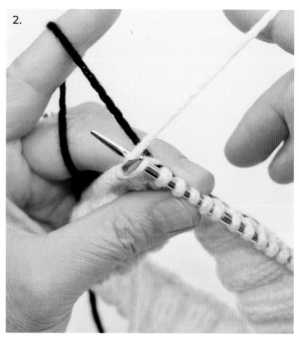

2.

Hold the new yarn in place with your left middle finger, and knit the next stitch as usual, locking in the new yarn.

3.

Complete the knit stitch.

4.

Put the right needle into the stitch as to knit and place the new yarn over the right needle.

5.

Wrap the working yarn around the right needle.

6.

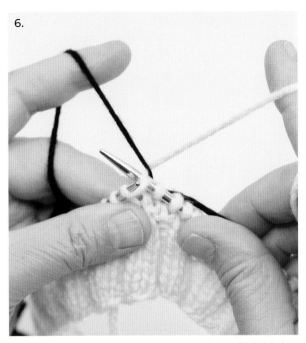

Move the new yarn (black) up and over the right needle, behind and away from the main color yarn (white).

7.

Finish the knit stitch.

8.

Knit the next stitch as usual, locking in the new yarn (black) with the main color yarn (white). Repeat Steps 4–8 three times. Knit to BOR marker. Now you are ready to knit with two colors.

4. KNIT COLORWORK PORTION OF COWL

Slip marker. Change to larger needles for the colorwork portion and work Round 1 of the chart (page 46) beginning with Stitch 1. Read the chart (page 46) from right to left, bottom to top. Repeat the chart nine times for a total of 144 stitches. Knit Rounds 1–16 of the chart. Follow the chart carefully on the first colorwork round to establish the pattern. Carry the CC in your left hand and the MC in your right hand. This is so that the pattern yarn is in the dominant position. Be consistent throughout the entire cowl. Repeat the chart one and a half times more, after completing Row 9 of the chart. Cut the CC yarn, leaving a 6-inch (15.25-cm) tail.

KNITTING WITH THE CONTRASTING COLOR IN THE LEFT HAND

1.

Starting position on the left of the stitch.

2.

Under the gate.

3.

Capture the (black) sheep.

4.

Back they come.

5.

And off they leap.

KNITTING WITH THE MAIN COLOR IN THE RIGHT HAND

1.

In through the front.

2.

Once . . .

3.

. . . around the back.

4.

Peek through the window.

5.

And off jumps Jack.

5. KNIT TWO ROUNDS IN MAIN COLOR AND DECREASE 4 STITCHES

With the MC, knit one round and weave out the tail from the CC (see the tutorial on weaving out on the following two pages). Switch to smaller needles and knit one round, decreasing 4 stitches evenly spaced by knitting 2 stitches together. *Knit 34 stitches then k2tog.* Work from * to * four times. Total stitches: 140.

WEAVING OUT THE CONTRASTING COLOR

1.

Put the CC yarn over the left needle.

2.

Wrap the MC around the right needle.

3.

Lift the CC off and away from the needle.

4.

Knit with the MC and pull the stitch through.

5.

Complete the stitch.

6.

Knit one as usual.

7.

Complete the stitch. Repeat the previous steps four times.

8.

Cut the CC yarn.

SANDER CHART

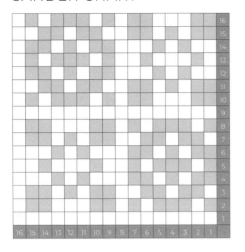

KEY

◻ = Main Color (MC)

▨ = Contrasting Color (CC)

6. WORK RIBBING

Switch to smaller needles and continue with the MC only, working 2x2 ribbing for nine rounds.

7. BIND OFF ALL STITCHES

Bind off with the following pattern: *k2, p2, k2, p2tog.* This may seem tricky, but all you do is bind off following the established ribbing pattern for the first 6 stitches (k2, p2, k2), then purl 2 stitches together while continuing to bind off. Repeat from * to * all the way around seventeen times. Finish the round with a k2, p2. Break the yarn and leave an 8-inch (20-cm) tail. Thread the tail of the yarn onto a tapestry needle. With a duplicate stitch, connect the last stitch of the round to the first stitch of the round.

8. FINISHING

Weave in all the ends, steam block your cowl, and wear or gift right away.

You can make a pair of Liv Mitts (page 29) with the leftover MC.

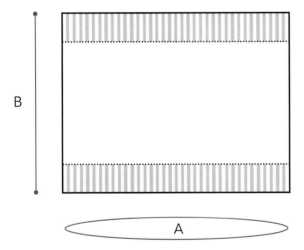

SANDER COWL SCHEMATIC

A- Circumference: 25 inches (63.5 cm)

B- Height: 8½ inches (21.5 cm)

SWEDISH LOVIKKA MITTENS

✿✿ ADVENTUROUS BEGINNER

Swedish Lovikka Mittens were created above the Arctic Circle in Lovikka, Sweden, by a young girl named Erika Aittamaa in 1892. They were made with heavy, Swedish wool, felted and combed to make them fluffy, then embroidered to make them festive. I designed my version for my daughter Anna to knit for friends while she recovered from an ice-skating injury when she was 14. In the process, she became a fabulous knitter. Because they are knit with one color, Lovikka Mittens are a great project for practicing whichever method of knitting is new to you. My version is made with soft, light, unspun Plötulopi wool from Iceland. You will love it. I hope you make these mittens for all your friends.

SKILLS YOU'LL PRACTICE

Long-tail cast on (page 184). Joining in the round seamlessly (page 37). Knitting with five double-pointed needles (DPNs)—if you are a beginning knitter, it can freak you out to knit with five needles at once, but take heart, it gets easier with practice. ssk decrease (page 186). Creating a thumbhole by knitting onto a scrap of yarn. Picking up stitches (page 186). Felting. Adding embroidered details with lazy daisy stitches (page 52), French knots (pages 53–54), and duplicate stitches (page 55).

SIZES

Women's S/M (Women's M/L, Men's M/L)

MATERIALS

YARN: Worsted | Ístex Plötulopi | 100% unspun Icelandic roving | 328 yards (300 m) per 3.5-ounce (100-g) skein | 1 skein [233 yards (195 m)] | Color: 001 (White)

YARN FOR EMBROIDERY: DK | Rauma Strikkegarn | 3-ply 100% Norwegian Wool | 114 yards (105 m) per 1.75-ounce (50-g) skein | 8 yards (7.5 m) for embroidery in each color | Colors: 151 (Blue), 131 (Gold), 128 (Red)

NEEDLES

NEEDLES: One set of double-pointed needles (DPNs) in size needed to obtain gauge. DPNs only. Don't magic loop. Don't use FlexiFlips.

SUGGESTED NEEDLE SIZE: US 7 (4.5 mm)

ADDITIONAL MATERIALS

Measuring tape, scissors, tapestry needle, scrap yarn, and wire brush

GAUGE AND SWATCH

12 stitches and 19 rounds = 4 inches (10 cm)

Felted to 13 stitches and 20 rounds = 4 inches (10 cm)

FINISHED MEASUREMENTS

WOMEN'S S/M: 4¼ inches (10.75 cm) wide and 9 inches (23 cm) long

WOMEN'S M/L: 4¼ inches (10.75 cm) wide and 9¾ inches (24.5 cm) long

MEN'S M/L: 4¾ inches (12 cm) wide and 11 inches (28 cm) long

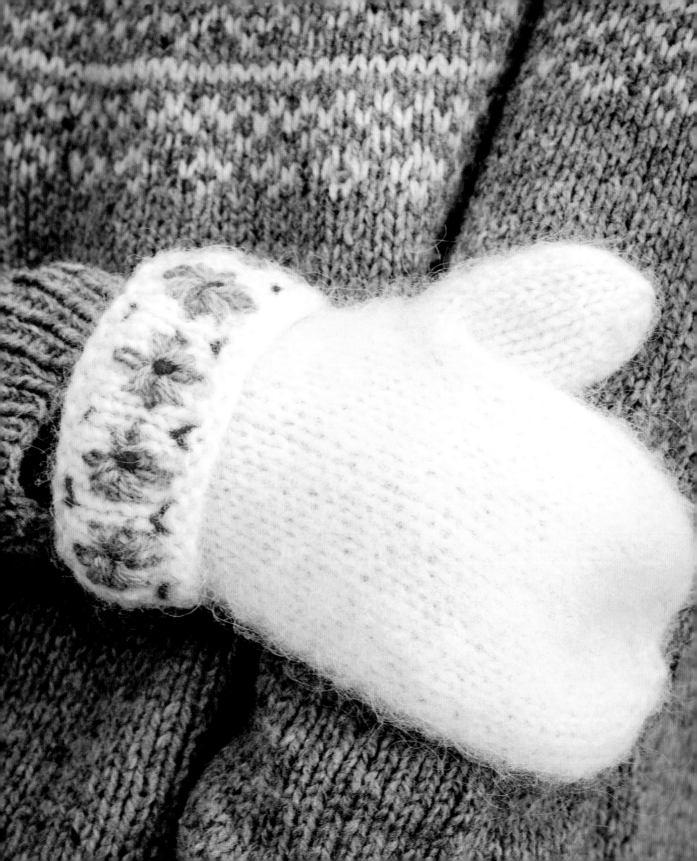

INSTRUCTIONS

1. CAST ON RIGHT-HAND MITTEN

With DPNs and two strands of white Icelandic unspun yarn, using a long-tail cast on, cast on 32 (32, 36) stitches. Divide the 32 (32, 36) stitches evenly onto four DPNs, 8 (8, 9) stitches on each needle.

2. JOIN TO WORK IN THE ROUND

Interlock the four needles to make a circle. Join to work in the round, being careful not to twist the cast-on stitches. Purl one round.

3. KNIT CUFF

Knit 9 (9, 10) rounds. Turn the work inside out and knit one round. This is a bit tricky because when you turn the work inside out, the first stitch of the round is directly on top of the last stitch of the previous round. Don't be alarmed by the tiny hole that exists from changing knitting directions. It will not show after the mitten is felted. Knit for 4 (4½, 5) inches [10 (11.5, 12.75) cm] from the cast on. Fold the cuff back, so that the RS stitches of the cuff are on the outside of the mitten.

4. KNIT FROM THE CUFF TO THE THUMB

Continue knitting until the mitten measures 4½ (5, 6) inches [11.5 (12.75, 15.25) cm] from the turning round to the base of the thumb. (Measure with the cuff folded.) If you would like a longer mitten, add additional rounds here.

5. SET ASIDE THE STITCHES FOR THE THUMB

Knit the first 7 stitches with a piece of scrap yarn for the stitches for the thumb. Then place the 7 stitches back onto the left needle.

6. CONTINUE KNITTING MITTEN

Continue knitting in the round with the Icelandic unspun for 4¼ (5, 6¼) inches [10.75 (12.75, 16) cm]. If you need a longer mitten, keep knitting the mitten until it measures 1 inch (2.5 cm) shorter than your desired length. Keep in mind that the mitten shrinks about 1 inch (2.5 cm) after felting.

7. SHAPE TOP OF MITTEN

Make sure there are 8 (8, 9) stitches on each of the four needles. Continue knitting, and at the end of each needle, ssk the last 2 stitches. Continue knitting in the round and decreasing the last 2 stitches until there is one stitch on each needle.

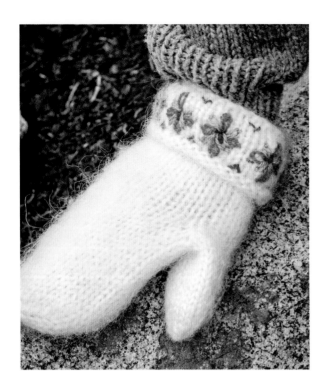

the back 7 stitches and pick up one stitch on the side. Total stitches: 16. Continue knitting in the round for 3½ (3¾, 5) inches [9 (9.5, 12.75) cm]. Divide the stitches onto four DPNs. Place 4 stitches on each needle. Knit across each needle until 2 stitches remain and ssk. Continue knitting in the round, decreasing on each needle until there is just one stitch on each needle. Break the yarn and thread a tapestry needle with both strands. Run the tapestry needle through the live stitches. Pull to gather. Insert the needle through the hole at the top of the thumb and pull to gather again. Run the tapestry needle through the live stitches again. Weave in the ends separately.

10. KNIT THE LEFT MITTEN

In this simple mitten pattern, the left is the same as the right mitten. Proceed confidently.

11. WASH

Wash the mittens on a quick cycle in your washing machine with mild soap and lukewarm water. Spin dry and then dry flat.

12. BRUSH

With a wire brush starting at the top of the mitten, brush the mitten from top to bottom. Always comb in the same direction. Turn the mitten inside out and brush the same way from the top of the mitten to the cuff. Do not brush the cuff stitches. Brush until your mitten is as soft and fuzzy as you would like.

13. EMBROIDER

With DK-weight yarn, embroider each cuff all the way around, with nine flowers made from lazy daisy stitches and French knots. Separate the flowers with duplicate stitches as indicated on the embroidery chart (page 51).

8. HOMESTRETCH

Break the yarn and leave a 6-inch (15.25-cm) tail. Thread a tapestry needle with both strands. With the tapestry needle, run both strands through the 4 live stitches. Pull to gather. Insert the needle through the hole at the top of the mitten. Turn the mitten inside out. Pull gently to gather and run the needle through the live stitches again. Weave in the ends separately at the top of the mitten. Weave in all other ends.

9. PICK UP THUMB STITCHES

Pull out the scrap yarn and transfer the 14 live thumb stitches onto two DPNs, 7 on each needle. With a third needle, knit across the first 7 stitches and pick up one stitch on the side of the thumb. Knit across

AMAZE YOUR FRIENDS: These mittens are so easy that you can memorize the entire pattern and knit mittens on the fly away from this book. Knitting without a pattern is a super happy life skill, and even a bit of a circus trick. Anyone have five pencils and some string? I can make you a pair of mittens while you watch.

LOVIKKA EMBROIDERY

 o – Red French Knot

 – Red Duplicate Stitch

 – Blue Lazy Daisy

 – Gold Lazy Daisy

LOVIKKA MITTEN SCHEMATIC

A- Hand circumference after felting: 8½ (8½, 9½) inches [22 (22, 24) cm]

B- Length of mitten after felting: 9 (9¾, 11) inches [23 (24.5, 28) cm]

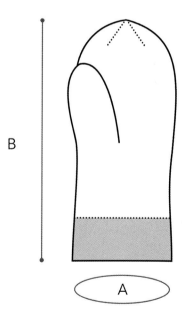

LAZY DAISY STITCH

1.

Come up through the center of the flower three times.

2.

Make a loop clockwise with the yarn and then with the tip of the needle, go back down through the center of the flower and come back up exactly where you want the top of the petal to be.

3.

Pull the yarn gently, catching the inside loop of the petal.

4.

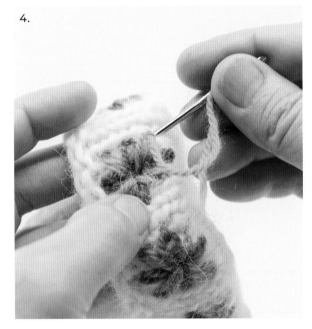

Make a small stitch over the top of the loop to secure the top of the petal.

5.

Pull gently to tighten the loop.

FRENCH KNOT

1.

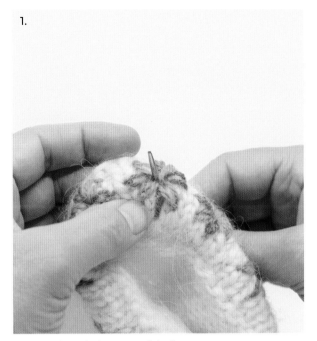

Come up through the center of the flower.

2.

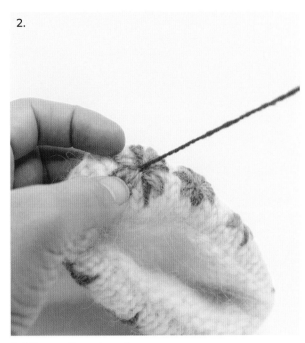

Pull the yarn through gently.

3.

Wrap the yarn . . .

4.

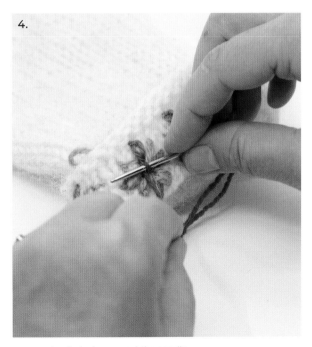

. . . counterclockwise around the needle . . .

5.

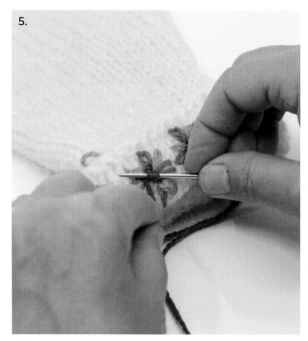

. . . three times.

6.

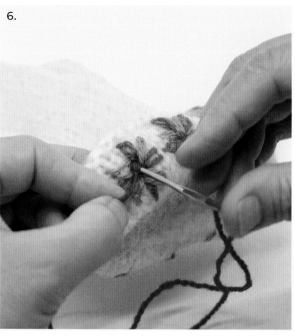

Insert the tip of the needle into the center of the flower (but not in the exact same spot as Step 1).

7.

With your thumb on the French knot to secure it, pull the needle through to the back of the work.

DUPLICATE STITCH

1.

Come up through the center of the base of a knit stitch.

2.

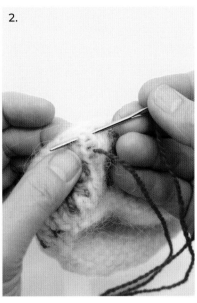

Bring the needle to the top of the right arm of the V of the stitch and go down through the hole just above the top of the right arm. Come out through the hole just above the top of the left arm. This runs the yarn behind the stitch above the one you're duplicating.

3.

Gently pull the yarn through to match the tension of the knit stitch.

4.

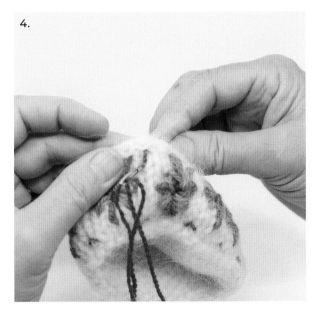

With the tip of the needle, go back down into the center of the base of the knit stitch.

5.

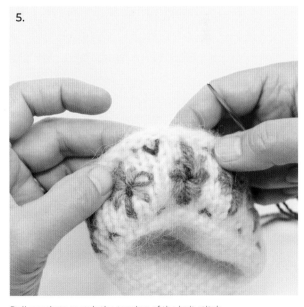

Pull gently to match the tension of the knit stitch.

LARS HAT

✳✳ ADVENTUROUS BEGINNER

This adorable hat is the simplest colorwork project in the book. The yarn is fat, the pattern is simple, and the hat works up in a flash. Another thing that makes Lars easy is that the colorwork is knit before the hat is shaped, so you can focus on the pattern first and then the decreases. No multitasking here. The Lars Hat is knit with Studio Donegal's Soft Donegal, then slightly felted to make it extra cozy. Switch the contrasting and main colors around, and you can make three or four hats with two skeins of yarn—now that's a lot of practice. You can become a hat factory and spread a little hat hygge to all your friends.

SKILLS YOU'LL PRACTICE

Long-tail cast on (page 184). Joining in the round seamlessly (page 37). Working 2x2 ribbing (k2, p2). Weaving a new yarn color in (and out) (pages 38–39 and 44–45). Knitting with two colors in the round, left and right together (pages 41–42). Reading a chart (page 9). Backward loop increase (page 182). K2tog decrease (page 184). Ssk decrease (page 186).

SIZES

Adult S (M, L)

M fits an average-sized head (22–24 inches [56–61 cm])

MATERIALS

YARN: Worsted | Studio Donegal's Soft Donegal | 100% merino wool | 207 yards (189 m) per 3.5-ounce (100-g) skein

MAIN COLOR (MC): 5207 (Snow) | 1 skein [75 yards (69 m)]

CONTRASTING COLOR (CC): 5221 (Rocky Paths) | 1 skein [40 yards (37 m)]

NEEDLES

NEEDLES: One 16-inch (40-cm) circular needle for the body and one set of double-pointed needles (DPNs) or FlexiFlips for the crown of the hat in size needed to obtain gauge

SUGGESTED NEEDLE SIZE: US 6 (4 mm)

ADDITIONAL MATERIALS

Stitch marker, scissors, tapestry needle, and snap-on pom-pom (optional)

GAUGE AND SWATCH

GAUGE: 20 stitches and 24 rows = 4 inches (10 cm)

Make a swatch in stranded colorwork and a swatch with a single color to find the perfect needle size.

FINISHED MEASUREMENTS

CIRCUMFERENCE: 18 (19¼, 20½) inches [45.5 (49, 52) cm]

LENGTH OF HAT FROM BRIM TO CROWN: 11½ (11¾, 11¾) inches [29 (30, 30) cm]

INSTRUCTIONS

1. CAST ON BRIM

With a 16-inch (40-cm) circular needle and the MC, using a long-tail cast on, cast on 88 (96, 104) stitches.

2. JOIN AND KNIT RIBBING

Join for working in the round, being careful not to twist the cast-on stitches. Round 1: Place a marker at the beginning of the round. *Knit 2, purl 2.* Repeat from * to * all the way around. Work the first 2 stitches with the working yarn and the tail from the long-tail cast on for a seamless join. (See the tutorial on page 37.) Continue in 2x2 ribbing for 5 inches (12.5 cm). For size small: Knit one round with MC and increase 2 stitches by adding a backward loop, twice, evenly spaced on the round. For size medium: Knit one round with MC. For size large: Knit one round with MC and decrease 2 stitches by k2tog twice, evenly spaced on the round. Total stitches: 90 (96, 102).

3. WORK BODY OF THE HAT INCLUDING COLORWORK

With the MC, knit 2 (2, 2) rounds.

Begin colorwork. Work Rounds 1–8 of Chart 1 (page 60). Read the chart from right to left, beginning with Stitch 1 of Round 1 of the chart. Chart 1 will be repeated 15 (16, 17) times. Keep the CC in the dominant position. If knitting with one color in each hand, hold the CC in the left hand and the MC in the right. If you are knitting with both colors in one hand, then place the CC to the left of the MC. Be consistent throughout the entire hat. When knitting with one color, knit with whichever hand you are most comfortable with.

For size small: Knit one round with MC decreasing 2 stitches by k2tog twice evenly spaced on the round. For size medium: With MC, knit one round. For size large: Knit one round with MC increasing 2 stitches by adding a backward loop, twice, evenly spaced on the round. Total stitches: 88 (96, 104).

With the MC, knit one round. Work Chart 2 (page 60), beginning with Stitch 1. Knit Rounds 1–4.

For size small: Knit one round with MC and increase 2 stitches by adding a backward loop, twice, evenly spaced on the round. For size medium: Knit one round with MC. For size large: Knit one round with MC and decrease 2 stitches by k2tog twice, evenly spaced on the round. Total stitches: 90 (96, 102).

With the MC, knit one round. Work Rounds 1–8 of Chart 1, beginning on Stitch 1.

For size small: Knit one round with MC and decrease 2 stitches by k2tog, twice, evenly spaced on the round. For size medium: Knit one round with MC. For size large: Knit one round with MC and increase 2 stitches by adding a backward loop, twice, evenly spaced on the round. Total stitches: 88 (96, 104).

4. BEGIN DECREASING FOR CROWN

Continuing with the MC, decrease every round as follows.

ROUND 1: *Ssk, knit 18 (20, 22) stitches, k2tog.* Repeat from * to * four times. Total stitches: 80 (88, 96).

ROUND 2: *Ssk, knit 16 (18, 20) stitches, k2tog.* Repeat from * to * four times. Total stitches: 72 (80, 88).

ROUND 3: *Ssk, knit 14 (16, 18) stitches, k2tog.* Repeat from * to * four times. Total stitches: 64 (72, 80).

ROUND 4: *Ssk, knit 12 (14, 16) stitches, k2tog.* Repeat from * to * four times. Total stitches: 56 (64, 72).

ROUND 5: *Ssk, knit 10 (12, 14) stitches, k2tog.* Repeat from * to * four times. Total stitches: 48 (56, 64).

ROUND 6: *Ssk, knit 8 (10, 12) stitches, k2tog.* Repeat from * to * four times. Total stitches: 40 (48, 56).

ROUND 7: *Ssk, knit 6 (8, 10) stitches, k2tog.* Repeat from * to * four times. Total stitches: 32 (40, 48).

ROUND 8: *Ssk, knit 4 (6, 8) stitches, k2tog.* Repeat from * to * four times. Total stitches: 24 (32, 40).

ROUND 9: *Ssk, knit 2 (4, 6) stitches, k2tog.* Repeat from * to * four times. Total stitches: 16 (24, 32). Size small skip to Row 12.

ROUND 10 (SIZES MEDIUM AND LARGE ONLY): *Ssk, knit - (2, 4) stitches, k2tog.* Repeat from * to * four times. Total stitches: - (16, 24). Size medium skip to Row 12.

ROUND 11 (SIZE LARGE ONLY): *Ssk, k2, k2tog.* Repeat from * to * four times. Total stitches: - (-, 16).

ROUND 12 (ALL SIZES): *Ssk, k2tog.* Repeat from * to * four times. Total stitches: 8 (8, 8).

ROUND 13: Knit one round.

Break the yarn, leaving a 6-inch (15.25-cm) tail. Thread the tail of the yarn onto a tapestry needle and through the remaining 8 live stitches and pull to close crown. Put the needle through the hole at the top of the hat. Pull to gather again. Run the tapestry needle through the live stitches again. Pull to gather. Weave in the tail.

5. FINISHING

Weave in the ends. Lightly felt by gently washing with lukewarm water on a speed cycle. Dry flat and steam block. Wear as is or sew on a snap for a pom-pom. Snap on the pom-pom. Wear or gift right away. Happy Winter!

LARS CHART 1   LARS CHART 2

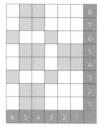

KEY

☐ = Main Color (MC)

☐ = Contrasting Color (CC)

LARS SCHEMATIC

A- Circumference at widest point: 18 (19¼, 20½) inches [45.5 (49, 52) cm]

B- Length of hat from brim to crown: 11½, (11¾, 11¾) inches [29 (30, 30) cm]

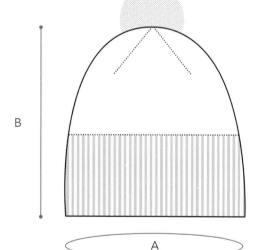

MAGNUS PULLOVER

✳ ✳ ADVENTUROUS BEGINNER

When people ask me what their first colorwork project should be, I always say, "Start with a sweater." Before I learned to knit, I always dreamed of making a Nordic sweater. Someday. Fortunately, I stumbled upon some Icelandic yarn in the Reykjavík airport when I was 19 and made a sweater as my very first project. I had found the perfect place to begin. Traditional Icelandic sweaters are knit in the round, bottom up, so they start out easy and slowly get more difficult. First, you practice knitting the body and sleeves in one color. The yarn is fat, so it grows fast. Then you put the body and the sleeves onto one needle and tackle the colorwork at the top as a reward. Magnus is a super comfy unisex sweater with a classic boyfriend fit. People won't believe it was your first project. But it absolutely can be!

SKILLS YOU'LL PRACTICE

Long-tail cast on (page 184). Duplicate stitch join (page 183). Joining in the round seamlessly (page 37). Working 2x2 ribbing (k2, p2). DPN work for the sleeves. Backward loop increase (page 182). Splicing yarn (page 186). Joining body and sleeves onto one needle. Weaving a new yarn color in (and out) (pages 38–39 and 44–45). Knitting with two colors in the round, left and right together (pages 41–42). Reading a chart (page 9). K2tog decrease (page 184). Ssk decrease (page 186). Mattress stitch (page 185).

SIZES

XS (S, M, L, XL, 2XL, 3XL, 4XL)

3–5 inches (7.75–12.75 cm) positive ease

MATERIALS

YARN: Worsted | Brooklyn Tweed Shelter | 100% American Targhee-Columbia Wool | 140 yards (128 m) per 1.75-ounce (50-g) skein

MAIN COLOR (MC): Snowbound | 6 (6, 7, 7, 8, 9, 10, 11) skeins [740 (810, 896, 960, 1064, 1232, 1372, 1512) yards] / [676 (740, 819, 877, 972, 1126, 1254, 1382) m]

CONTRASTING COLOR 1 (CC1): Soot | 1 skein [78 (84, 90, 96, 102, 108, 114, 120) yards] / [71 (77, 82, 88, 93, 99, 104, 110) m]

CONTRASTING COLOR 2 (CC2): Truffle Hunt | 1 skein [65 (68, 70, 73, 75, 78, 80, 83) yards] / [60 (62, 64, 66, 69, 71, 73, 76) m]

CONTRASTING COLOR 3 (CC3): Fossil | 1 skein [95 (102, 107, 112, 117, 123, 128, 132) yards / 86 (93, 98, 102, 107, 112, 117, 121) m]

NEEDLES: One 32-inch (80-cm) or 40-inch (100-cm) circular needle for the body and one set of double-pointed needles (DPNs), FlexiFlips, or a 16-inch (40-cm) circular needle for the sleeves in size needed to obtain gauge in colorwork and single color

SUGGESTED NEEDLE SIZE: US 9 (5.5 mm)

One 32-inch (80-cm) or 40-inch (100-cm) circular needle one size smaller than gauge-size needle and one set of double-pointed needles (DPNs) or FlexiFlips to use for the ribbing

SUGGESTED NEEDLE SIZE: US 8 (5 mm)

GAUGE AND SWATCH

16 stitches and 20 rounds = 4 inches (10 cm)

Please swatch in the round to determine needle size.

FINISHED MEASUREMENTS

CHEST: 36 (40, 43, 46, 49, 52, 55, 58) inches [91.5 (101.5, 109.25, 117, 124.5, 132, 139.75, 147.5) cm]

BODY LENGTH TO UNDERARM: 16 (16½, 17, 18, 19, 20, 21, 21) inches [40.5 (42, 43, 45.5, 48.5, 51, 53.5, 53.5) cm]

SLEEVE LENGTH: 18 (18½, 19, 19, 20, 20, 21½, 21½) inches [45.5 (47, 48.5, 48.5, 51, 51, 54.5, 54.5) cm]

YOKE DEPTH: 9½ (9½, 9½, 9¾, 10, 10¼, 10½, 10½) inches [24 (24, 24, 24.5, 25.5, 26, 26.5, 26.5) cm]

TOTAL LENGTH: 25½ (26, 26½, 27¾, 29, 30¼, 31½, 31½) inches [65 (66, 67.5, 70.5, 73.5, 76.75, 80, 80) cm]

INSTRUCTIONS

1. CAST ON

With smaller needles and MC, using a long-tail cast on, cast on 144 (160, 172, 184, 196, 208, 220, 232) stitches.

2. RIBBING

Place a marker at the beginning of the round. Join by knitting from the last cast-on stitch to the first cast-on stitch for working in the round. Be careful not to twist the cast-on stitches. Work the first 2 stitches with the working yarn and the tail from the long-tail cast on for a seamless join. (See the tutorial on page 37.)

ROUND 1: *Knit 2, purl 2.* Repeat from * to * all the way around. Work 2x2 ribbing for another seventeen rounds.

ADDITIONAL MATERIALS

Stitch markers, measuring tape, scissors, and tapestry needle

NOTE: Swatch in both one color and in colorwork. You may need to knit the single-color part of the sweater with a smaller needle than the colorwork section. The gauge is the same throughout the sweater.

3. KNIT BODY

Knit onto larger gauge-size needles and knit in the round until the body measures 16 (16½, 17, 18, 19, 20, 21, 21) inches [40.5 (42, 43, 45.5, 48.5, 51, 53.5, 53.5) cm] or until the desired length from the beginning of the ribbing to the underarm. Stop knitting 4 (5, 5, 5, 5, 6, 6, 6) stitches before the marker. Bind off the next 8 (10, 10, 10, 10, 12, 12, 12) stitches for the underarm. To knit smoothly from one skein to the next, always splice the ends together. See the tutorial on page 186.

4. KNIT SLEEVE

With smaller DPNs and the MC, cast on 40 (40, 40, 44, 44, 48, 48, 52) stitches. Divide stitches evenly between three DPNs. Place a marker and join by knitting from the last cast-on stitch to the first cast-on stitch. Work in 2x2 ribbing (k2, p2) for 2½ inches (6.5 cm). Next round, change to larger needles. Knit 2½ inches (6.5 cm) farther. On the next round, increase with backward loop one stitch right after the first stitch and before the last stitch of the round. Total stitches: 42 (42, 42, 46, 46, 50, 50, 54). For all sizes, increase 2 stitches in the same manner every 2 inches (5 cm) 3 (5, 6, 5, 6, 7, 8, 7) more times. Total sleeve stitches: 48 (52, 54, 56, 58, 64, 66, 68). Continue knitting until the sleeve measures 18 (18½, 19, 19, 20, 20, 21½, 21½) inches [45.5 (47, 48.5, 48.5, 51, 51, 54.5, 54.5) cm] or the desired length to underarm. On the last round, stop knitting 4 (5, 5, 5, 5, 6, 6, 6) stitches before the marker. Bind off the next 8 (10, 10, 10, 10, 12, 12, 12) stitches for underarm.

5. JOIN BODY TO FIRST SLEEVE FOR THE YOKE

Match up the stitches set aside for the underarm on the body to the stitches set aside for the underarm on the sleeve. Place a marker on the tip of the needle with the body stitches to mark the beginning of the round. Continuing with the yarn that was used for knitting the body, knit across the 40 (42, 44, 46, 48, 52, 54, 56) left-sleeve stitches. Knit across the front of the body for 64 (70, 76, 82, 88, 92, 98, 104) stitches. Place the next 8 (10, 10, 10, 10, 12, 12, 12) stitches on a holder for the underarm.

6. KNIT SECOND SLEEVE

Repeat Step 4 and knit the second sleeve.

7. JOIN SECOND SLEEVE TO THE BODY

Match up the stitches set aside for the right underarm on the body to the stitches set aside for the underarm on the right sleeve. Knit from the front stitches to the right sleeve for 40 (42, 44, 46, 48, 52, 54, 56) stitches. Place marker B. Continue knitting across the 64 (70, 76, 82, 88, 92, 98, 104) stitches for the back of the sweater to marker A. You have joined the sleeves to the body and are ready to knit the yoke. Total stitches: 208 (224, 240, 256, 272, 288, 304, 320). Knit 4 (5, 5, 6, 7, 8, 9, 10) rounds.

> **NOTE:** The marker A is placed at the beginning of the round and is located at the back of the left shoulder of the sweater.

garment. You can make Magnus with or without short rows. It's up to you. To work short rows, you will be adding two German short rows from shoulder to shoulder across the back. With the MC, beginning at marker A, knit across 15 (16, 17, 17, 18, 19, 20, 21) left-sleeve stitches. Work a German short row (GSR): Turn work. Bring your working yarn to the front and, with the tip of the right needle, slip the first stitch off the left needle to the right needle, tug the working yarn and bring it over the top of the left needle, creating a double stitch. Bring the working yarn between the two needles to the front and purl across to marker B and across 15 (16, 17, 17, 18, 19, 20, 21) right-sleeve stitches. Turn and bring the yarn to the front of the work and, with the tip of the right needle, slip the first stitch to the right needle. Pull on the working yarn over the right needle to the back. Knit one row, stopping 3 stitches before the double stitch created by the GSR. Work a GSR. Purl to 3 stitches before the double stitch created by the GSR. Work a GSR. Knit across the back stitches until you reach the marker at the beginning of the round.

8. KNIT THE YOKE

Now the fun starts. Carry the CC in your left hand and the MC in your right hand (making sure that the CC is in the dominant position). Work the knitting chart (page 67) beginning at the right bottom corner. Repeat the chart 26 (28, 30, 32, 34, 36, 38, 40) times. Work Rows 1–41 of the chart. Rows 20, 26, 33, 36, and 38 are decrease rounds. Work the decrease in the background color and decrease by knitting the 2 stitches marked with dots together with a ssk.

9. WORK SHORT ROWS (OPTIONAL)

Traditional Icelandic sweaters didn't have short rows. Short rows are added to improve the fit of the sweater by lowering the neckline in the front of the

10. WORK NECKBAND

Now there are 78 (84, 90, 96, 102, 108, 114, 120) stitches. Knit one round, knitting the double stitches together from the short rows on the sleeves as you come to them. At the same time, adjust the stitch count as noted for each size by decreasing one stitch with a k2tog 2 (0, 2, 0, 2, 0, 2, 0) times evenly spaced. Total neckband stitches: 76 (84, 88, 96, 100, 108, 112, 120).

Work 2x2 ribbing (k2, p2) for five rounds. Bind off all stitches following the established ribbing pattern. Break yarn, leaving an 8-inch (20-cm) tail. Thread the tail of the yarn onto a tapestry needle. With a duplicate stitch, connect the last stitch of the round to the first stitch of the round.

MAGNUS CHART

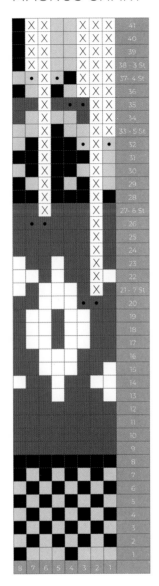

11. FINISHING

Weave in all the ends and graft together the underarm stitches. Steam block. Congrats! If you knit this for your boyfriend, feel free to borrow it.

MAGNUS SCHEMATIC

A- Chest circumference: 36 (40, 43, 46, 49, 52, 55, 58) inches [91.5 (101.5, 109.25, 117, 124.5, 132, 139.75, 147.5) cm]

B- Body length to underarm: 16 (16½, 17, 18, 19, 20, 21, 21) inches [40.5 (42, 43, 45.5, 48.5, 51, 53.5, 53.5) cm]

C- Sleeve length: 18 (18½, 19, 19, 20, 20, 21½, 21½) inches [45.5 (47, 48.5, 48.5, 51, 51, 54.5, 54.5) cm]

D- Yoke depth: 9½ (9½, 9½, 9¾, 10, 10¼, 10½, 10½) inches [24 (24, 24, 24.5, 25.5, 26, 26.5, 26.5) cm]

E- Total length: 25½ (26, 26½, 27¾, 29, 30¼, 31½, 31½) inches [65 (66, 67.5, 70.5, 73.5, 76.75, 80, 80) cm]

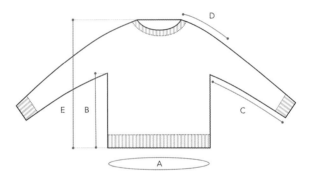

KEY

x = No stitch

• = Decrease by knitting the two dots together

□ = Contrasting Color 3 (CC3)

□ = Main Color (MC)

■ = Contrasting Color 2 (CC2)

■ = Contrasting Color 1 (CC1)

MAJA PULLOVER

✴✴ ADVENTUROUS BEGINNER

Maja is the perfect cozy weekend sweater. Absolutely easy enough to be your first knit, yet so classic that you'll still be wearing it twenty years from now. The extra deep Icelandic yoke draws on iconic X and O Setesdal motifs to create a whimsical blend of Norwegian and Icelandic knitting traditions. As with the Magnus Pullover (page 63), you can literally learn to knit on this sweater. The construction is simple—you basically knit a split hem, join the hems together, and continue in the round to knit a tube for the body and two more tubes for the sleeves. The colorwork fun begins before you join the sleeves to the body and knit the yoke. As the yoke grows, the rows get shorter and shorter. Before you know it, it's a sweater. You bind off the neck, graft the underarms together, steam block, and wear it immediately. There's no sewing, no fuss. Just sweater making in its easiest form with beautiful motifs that have been knit in Norway for centuries.

SKILLS YOU'LL PRACTICE

Long-tail cast on (page 184). Duplicate stitch join (page 183). Joining in the round seamlessly (page 37). Working 1x1 ribbing (k1, p1) with a split hem. DPN work for the sleeves. Backward loop increase (page 182). Splicing yarn (page 186). Joining body and sleeves onto one needle. Weaving a new yarn color in (and out) (pages 38–39 and 44–45). Knitting with two colors in the round, left and right together (pages 41–42). Reading a chart (page 9). K2tog decrease (page 184). Ssk decrease (page 186). Mattress stitch (page 185).

SIZES

XS (S, M, L, XL, 2XL, 3XL, 4XL)

3–5 inches (7.5–13 cm) positive ease

MATERIALS

YARN: Worsted | Brooklyn Tweed Shelter | 100% American Targhee-Columbia Wool | 140 yards (128 m) per 1.75-ounce (50-g) skein

MAIN COLOR (MC): Sweatshirt | 6 (7, 7, 8, 9, 10, 11, 12) skeins [812 (910, 970, 1050, 1218, 1320, 1450, 1610) yards] / [742 (832, 886, 960, 1113, 1207, 1325, 1472) m]

CONTRASTING COLOR (CC): Fossil | 2 (2, 2, 3, 3, 3, 3, 3) skeins [234 (252, 270, 288, 306, 324, 342, 360) yards] / [213 (230, 246, 263, 280, 296, 312, 329) m]

NEEDLES: One 32-inch (80-cm) or 40-inch (100-cm) circular needle for the body and one set of double-pointed needles (DPNs), FlexiFlips, or a 16-inch (40-cm) circular needle for the sleeves in size needed to obtain gauge in colorwork and single color

SUGGESTED NEEDLE SIZE: US 9 (5.5 mm)

One 32-inch (80-cm) or 40-inch (100-cm) circular needle one size smaller than gauge-size needle and one set of DPNs or FlexiFlips to use for the ribbing

SUGGESTED NEEDLE SIZE: US 8 (5 mm)

ADDITIONAL MATERIALS

Stitch marker, measuring tape, scissors, and tapestry needle

GAUGE AND SWATCH

16 stitches and 20 rounds = 4 inches (10 cm)

Please swatch in the round to determine needle size.

> **NOTE:** Swatch in both one color and in colorwork. You may need to knit the single-color part of the sweater with a smaller needle than the colorwork section. The gauge is the same throughout the sweater.

FINISHED MEASUREMENTS

CHEST: 37 (40, 43, 46, 49, 52, 55, 58) inches [94 (101.5, 109.25, 117, 124.5, 132, 139.75, 147.5) cm]

BODY LENGTH TO UNDERARM: 15¼ (15½, 16, 16½, 17, 18¼, 20, 21¼) inches [39 (39.5, 40.5, 42, 43, 46.5, 51, 54) cm] from hem

SLEEVE LENGTH: 18 (18½, 19, 19, 19½, 20, 20, 20¾) inches [46 (47, 48.25, 48.25, 49.5, 51, 51, 53) cm]

YOKE DEPTH: 9½ (9½, 9½, 9½, 10¾, 10¾, 10¾, 10¾) inches [24 (24, 24, 24, 27, 27, 27, 27) cm]

TOTAL LENGTH: 24¾ (25, 25½, 26, 27¾, 29, 30¾, 32) inches [63 (63.5, 64.75, 66, 70.5, 73.5, 78, 81.25) cm]

INSTRUCTIONS

1. CAST ON BACK HEM

With smaller needles and MC, using a long-tail cast on, cast on 75 (81, 87, 93, 99, 105, 111, 117) stitches.

2. WORK BACK HEM AND FRONT HEM SEPARATELY

ROW 1 (RS): *Knit 1, purl 1.* Repeat from * to * across row until one stitch remains. Knit last stitch.

ROW 2 (WS): *Purl 1, knit 1.* Repeat from * to * across row until one stitch remains. Purl last stitch.

Repeat Rows 1 and 2 to work 1x1 ribbing for 3 inches (7.5 cm). End after completing a wrong side row of the back hem. (The WS will start and end with a purl stitch.) Don't turn work. Break yarn leaving a 6-inch (15.25-cm) tail.

With the same needle and the WS of the back hem facing toward you, hold the needle with the back hem in the right hand and long-tail cast on 75 (81, 87, 93, 99, 105, 111, 117) stitches for the front hem. Turn (RS). Work Row 1: *Knit 1, purl 1.* Repeat from * to * across row until one stitch remains. Knit last stitch. Turn (WS). Work Row 2: *Purl 1, knit 1.* Repeat from * to * across row until one stitch remains. Purl last stitch. Work 1x1 ribbing until the front hem measures 2½ inches (6.5 cm), and after completing a wrong side row of the hem. (The WS will begin and end with a purl stitch.)

3. JOIN FRONT AND BACK HEM TO WORK IN THE ROUND

Turn (RS) and work 1x1 ribbing until the last stitch of the front hem. With the last stitch of the front hem and the first stitch from the back hem, join the front hem to the back hem with k2tog. Work 1x1 ribbing across the back hem until the last stitch of the back hem. Join the back to the front by knitting the last stitch of the back hem to the first stitch of the front hem with ssk. Place a marker at the beginning of the round. Working in the round, knit one row. Total stitches: 148 (160, 172, 184, 196, 208, 220, 232).

4. KNIT BODY

Knit onto larger gauge-size needles and knit in the round until the body measures 13½ (13¾, 14¼, 14¾, 15¼, 16½, 18¼, 19½) inches [34.5 (35, 36.25, 37.5, 38.75, 42, 46.5, 49.5) cm] or until the body is 1¾ inches (4.5 cm) shorter than the desired length from the bottom of the hem to the underarm. Measure from the bottom of the front hem for this measurement. To knit smoothly from one skein to the next, always splice the ends together. See the tutorial on page 186.

5. NOW THE FUN STARTS

Carry the CC in your left hand and the MC in your right hand (making sure that the contrasting color is in the dominant position) and begin knitting Chart 1 (page 74) on Stitch 1 of Round 1. Knit Rounds 1–7. At the end of Round 7, break the MC and knit Round 8 with the CC (weaving in the tail of the MC). Knit to the end of the round and then slip the previous 4 (5, 5, 5, 5, 6, 6, 6) stitches of Round 8 back onto the left needle. With the MC, knit and bind off the following 8 (10, 10, 10, 10, 12, 12, 12) stitches for the underarm. Break the yarn, leaving a 6-inch (15.25-cm) tail on each side for sewing later. Body measures 15¼ (15½, 16, 16½, 17, 18¼, 20, 21¼) inches [38.75 (39.5, 40.5, 42, 43, 46.5, 51, 54) cm] from front hem cast on.

6. KNIT SLEEVE

With smaller DPNs and the MC, cast on 40 (40, 42, 42, 44, 48, 48, 50) stitches. Divide the stitches evenly between three DPNs. Place a marker and join by knitting from the last cast-on stitch to the first cast-on stitch. Work the first 2 stitches with the working yarn and the tail from the long-tail cast on for a seamless join. (See the tutorial on page 37.) Round 1: *Knit 1, purl 1.* Work from * to * around sleeve. Work 1x1 ribbing for fifteen rounds.

(weaving in the tail of the MC). When Round 8 is completed, slip the last 4 (5, 5, 5, 5, 6, 6, 6) stitches of Round 8 back onto the left needle. With the MC yarn, knit and bind off the next 8 (10, 10, 10, 10, 12, 12, 12) stitches for the underarm. Break yarn, leaving a 6-inch (15.25-cm) tail on each side for sewing later.

7. JOIN BODY TO THE LEFT SLEEVE FOR THE YOKE

Match up the stitches set aside for the underarm on the body to the stitches set aside for the underarm on the sleeve. Place a marker. With a new MC skein, knit the left sleeve for 40 (42, 44, 46, 48, 52, 54, 56) stitches. Knit across the front of the body for 66 (70, 76, 82, 88, 92, 98, 104) stitches. This MC round is technically Round 1 of Chart 2 (2, 2, 2, 3, 3, 3, 3).

Bind off the next 8 (10, 10, 10, 10, 12, 12, 12) stitches for the right underarm. Break yarn. You are all ready to attach the second sleeve. Set work aside.

8. KNIT THE SECOND SLEEVE

Repeat Step 6 to knit the right sleeve.

9. JOIN SECOND SLEEVE TO THE BODY

Match up the stitches for the right underarm on the sleeve to the underarm stitches on the body. With the MC, knit 40 (42, 44, 46, 48, 52, 54, 56) right-sleeve stitches. Continue knitting across the 66 (70, 76, 82, 88, 92, 98, 104) stitches to the marker. Congrats! You have joined the sleeves to the body and are ready to knit the yoke. Total stitches: 212 (224, 240, 256, 272, 288, 304, 320).

> **NOTE:** The marker is placed at the beginning of the round and is located at the back of the left shoulder of the sweater.

On the next round, with larger, gauge-size needles, knit in the round for 4 inches (10 cm). On the next round, increase one stitch right after the first stitch and before the last stitch of the round. Total stitches: 42 (42, 44, 44, 46, 50, 50, 52). Increase 2 stitches in the same manner every 2 (2, 2, 1¾, 1¾, 1½, 1½, 1½) inches [5 (5, 5, 4.5, 4.5, 4, 4, 4) cm] and repeat 3 (5, 6, 6, 7, 7, 9, 8) times. Total stitches: 48 (52, 56, 56, 60, 64, 68, 68). Continue knitting until the sleeve measures 16¼ (16¾, 17¼, 17¼, 17¾, 18¼, 18¼, 19) inches [41.5 (42.5, 44, 44, 45, 46.5, 46.5, 48.5) cm] or 1¾ inches (4.5 cm) short of desired sleeve length. Beginning on Stitch 1 of Round 1 on Chart 1, work Rounds 1–6. Work Round 7, and for sizes M, XL, and 3XL work Round 7 and decrease 2 stitches by k2tog twice, evenly spaced on the round. Total stitches: 48 (52, 54, 56, 58, 64, 66, 68). For all sizes, at the end of Round 7, break MC and knit Round 8 with the CC

10. KNIT THE YOKE

Start Round 2 of Chart 2 (2, 2, 2, 3, 3, 3, 3) (page 74). Repeat the chart 13 (14, 15, 16, 17, 18, 19, 20) times on each round. For XS only, see note below. Continue following Chart 2 (2, 2, 2, 3, 3, 3, 3). Rounds 28, 30, 35, 41, and 47 on Chart 2 and Rounds 34, 36, 41, 47, and 53 on Chart 3 are the decrease rounds. Work the decrease as indicated on the charts by knitting the 2 stitches marked with dots together with ssk for the first decrease and k2tog for the second decrease on each decrease round.

NOTE: For size XS only, 4 stitches need to be decreased on Round 2. The decrease will happen at the place where the sleeve meets the body. Using the last stitch of Round 1 and the first stitch of Round 2, k2tog. Keeping pattern correct, knit across the left sleeve, and with the last stitch of the sleeve and the first stitch of the front body, ssk. Knit across the body, and with the last stitch of the body and the first stitch of the right sleeve, k2tog. Knit across the right shoulder, and with the last stitch of the sleeve and the first stitch of the body, ssk. Four stitches have been decreased. Knit to the end of the round. Total stitches: 208 (224, 240, 256, 272, 288, 304, 320).

11. WORK NECKBAND

There are now 78 (84, 90, 96, 102, 108, 114, 120) stitches on the needle. With the MC and smaller needles, knit one row. Work 1x1 ribbing (k1, p1) for five rounds. Bind off all stitches following the established 1x1 ribbing pattern. Break yarn, leaving an 8-inch (20-cm) tail. Thread the tail of the yarn onto a tapestry needle. With a duplicate stitch, connect the last stitch of the round to the first stitch of the round.

12. FINISHING

Weave in all the ends and sew the underarm stitches together with a mattress stitch. Steam block. Congrats! Book your tickets to Norway. You have the right sweater for the trip.

MAJA SCHEMATIC

A- Chest circumference: 37 (40, 43, 46, 49, 52, 55, 58) inches [94 (101.5, 109.25, 117, 124.5, 132, 139.75, 147.5) cm]

B- Body length to underarm: 15¼ (15½, 16, 16½, 17, 18¼, 20, 21¼) inches [39 (39.5, 40.5, 42, 43, 46.5, 51, 54) cm] from front hem.

C- Sleeve length: 18 (18½, 19, 19, 19½, 20, 20, 20¾) inches [46 (47, 48.25, 48.25, 49.5, 51, 51, 53) cm]

D- Yoke depth: 9½ (9½, 9½, 9½, 10¾, 10¾, 10¾, 10¾) inches [24 (24, 24, 24, 27, 27, 27, 27) cm]

E- Total length measured from front cast on to neck band: 24¾ (25, 25½, 26, 27¾, 29, 30¾, 32) inches [63 (63.5, 64.75, 66, 70.5, 73.5, 78, 81.25) cm]

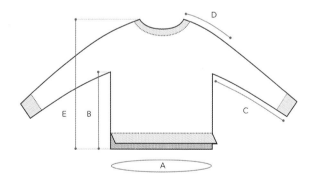

KEY (CHARTS ON PAGE 74)

| X | = No stitch |

• = Decrease by knitting the two dots together

= Contrasting Color (CC)

= Main Color (MC)

MAJA CHART 1

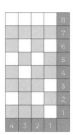

MAJA CHART 2

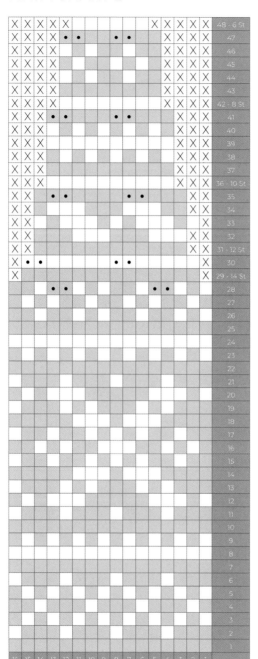

MAJA CHART 3

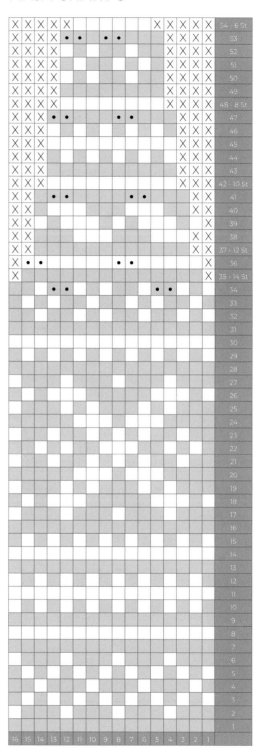

FREJA HAT

✺✺ ADVENTUROUS BEGINNER

If you are new to colorwork, start with one of the simpler projects in this chapter and then you will be ready for Freja. Even though this hat involves full-on, small-scale colorwork, it's also a little project that was carefully designed for easy knitting. Freja is an excellent bridge from the simple projects in Chapter 1 to the more complicated projects in Chapter 2.

Named after the Norse goddess of love, Freja's crown has five stars that form a snowflake. The brim is circled with hearts that represent love and courage. It features two traditional Norwegian XO (Kors og Kringle) patterns. The X represents the St. Andrew's Cross and the O is the pagan symbol for the sun. I love that Norwegians use Christian and pagan symbols side-by-side. To me, Xs and Os also carry a hidden message. When our kids were little, I told them that I knit Xs and Os in their clothing to remind them that I love them. When they were far from home, they could look down at their sweater or mittens and know they were loved. I hope you make this hat twice, once for yourself and again for someone you adore.

SKILLS YOU'LL PRACTICE

Long-tail cast on (page 184). Joining in the round seamlessly (page 37). Working 1x1 colorwork ribbing (k1, p1). Weaving a new yarn color in (and out) (pages 38–39 and 44–45). Knitting with two colors in the round, left and right together (pages 41–42). Reading a chart (page 9). Sl1-k2tog-psso decrease (page 186).

SIZE

One size only. Fits average-sized head [22–24 inches (56–61 cm)]. You may alter needle size to make a slightly larger or smaller hat.

MATERIALS

YARN: Sport | Rauma Tumi | 50% Alpaca 50% Norwegian Wool | 142 yards (130 m) per 1.75-ounce (50-g) skein

MAIN COLOR (MC): SFN10 (White) | 1 skein [71 yards (65 m)]

CONTRASTING COLOR (CC): 7255 (Mustard) | 1 skein [71 yards (65 m)]

NEEDLES: One 16-inch (40-cm) circular needle and one set of DPNs or FlexiFlips in size needed to obtain gauge

SUGGESTED NEEDLE SIZE: US 3 (3.25 mm)

One 16-inch (40-cm) circular needle one size smaller than gauge-size needle

SUGGESTED NEEDLE SIZE: US 2 (2.75 mm)

ADDITIONAL MATERIALS

Stitch marker, scissors, and tapestry needle

GAUGE AND SWATCH

GAUGE: 26 stitches and 31 rows = 4 inches (10 cm)

FINISHED MEASUREMENTS

CIRCUMFERENCE: 18½ inches (47 cm) (unstretched)

LENGTH OF HAT FROM THE BRIM TO THE CROWN:
7¾ inches (19.5 cm)

INSTRUCTIONS

1. CAST ON BRIM

With smaller needles and MC, using a long-tail cast on, cast on 120 stitches.

2. JOIN AND KNIT RIBBING

Join for knitting in the round, being careful not to twist the cast-on stitches. Place a marker at the beginning of the round. (Hint: Work the first 2 stitches with the working yarn and the tail from the long-tail cast on for a seamless join.) Make sure on the next round to treat the first 2 stitches after the join as 2 stitches (not 4) by knitting the working yarn and the tail together as one stitch. Round 1: *Knit 1, purl 1.* Repeat from * to * all the way around. Total stitches: 120.

3. BEGIN COLORWORK

Continue working 1x1 ribbing, reading the chart (page 79) from right to left, bottom to top. Begin with Stitch 1 of Round 1. Rounds 1–4: The knit stitches in the ribbing are worked with the CC and the purl stitches are worked with the MC. Rounds 5–8: Continue with the colorwork pattern but all the stitches are knit. Round 9: Switch to larger needles and follow the chart. There will be five repeats of the chart on each round.

Knit through Round 38 on the chart. Do not knit the last stitch of the round.

4. BEGIN DECREASING FOR CROWN ROUNDS 39–60

On Round 38 of the chart, begin the decreases for the crown. The 24-stitch repeat is worked five times across the round, so there will be five star patterns at the top of the crown. Pay attention to the stitch count on the right side of the chart. Heads up: The decreases are worked in between each of the star motifs. This is a bit tricky at the beginning of the round, because you use the last stitch of the round before the decrease round for the slip stitch. I am using the decrease to hide the inherent jog that happens in knitting in the round. For example, for the first decrease on Round 39, the last stitch of Round 38 is slipped and then Stitch 1 and 2 of Round 39 are knit together, then the slipped stitch from Round 38 is passed over Stitch 1 (and 2) on Round 39. After that, 21 stitches are worked in pattern, and then the last stitch (Stitch 24) is slipped in preparation to be passed over the next 2 stitches that are knit together on the next repeat.

(Step 4 continued)

On Round 39 of the chart, Stitch 2 and Stitch 24 (and all decreased stitches on the following rounds) are noted with a "no-stitch" on the chart. The sl1-k2tog-psso decrease uses the stitch before and after Stitch 1 on the chart. After the first pattern repeat, the following four pattern repeats are worked by a standard sl1-k2tog-psso decrease between the heart motifs. On the last pattern repeat on Round 39, work the sl1-k2tog-psso decrease, then knit the 21 stitches in pattern. Notice that there isn't a Stitch 24 to slip because the last stitch has already been slipped from Round 38 and used for the first decrease. Knit Round 40 following the chart. Continue working Rounds 41–59 in the same manner, following the chart carefully, decreasing every other round. Decrease rounds are on odd Rounds 39, 41, 43, 45, 47, 49, 51, 53, 55, 57, and 59. Final stitch count is 10. Break the yarn, leaving a 6-inch (15.25-cm) tail. Thread the tail of the yarn onto a tapestry needle and through the remaining 10 live stitches and pull to close crown.

5. FINISHING

Weave in the ends. Hand wash and rinse in lukewarm water. Roll up into a towel to remove excess water. Steam block and dry flat. Wear right away and start knitting another for someone you love.

FREJA CHART

FREJA SCHEMATIC

A- Circumference at the widest point: 18½ inches (47 cm)

B- Length from brim to crown: 7¾ inches (19.5 cm)

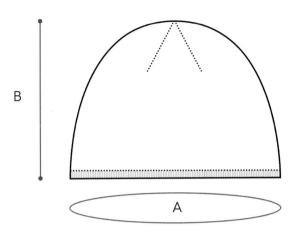

KEY

x	= No stitch
•	= Purl
⋀	= sl1-k2tog-psso
	= Main Color (MC)
▨	= Contrasting Color (CC)

MIND THE GAP

LEARN TO CATCH FLOATS WITH MORE INTRICATE NORDIC COLORWORK

Make something wonderful while you practice another critical colorwork skill: catching floats. When a pattern calls for you to switch colors every few stitches, you don't really need to worry about the back side of your work. But if you have to carry a color for six or more stitches in a row, the color you are not knitting with will create long strands or "floats" of yarn along the back side. These long floats can be problematic. They get caught on fingers and buttons. They can snag the fabric. They sometimes even inhibit the stretch of the finished garment. However, if floats are caught and woven into the knitting as you go (without showing through to the front) they become a natural part of the fabric.

Except for catching floats, the cozy Scandinavian projects in this chapter are not much more difficult than the chapter before. You don't even need to capture floats on every round. Just a few here and there. Once again, you can pick any project that truly speaks to you to learn your new skill. Choose the lovely top-down knitted sweater inspired by Norwegian rosemåling. Or the jumper with a yoke of modern tulips. Make the cowl that incorporates the famous Setesdal pattern. Or choose the timeless Dagna Hat (page 95). You can even make a mother-and-daughter pair of bright floral yoke sweaters that capture the joy of Swedish Midsommar.

Whatever project you choose, make sure you read the float-catching tutorial included in the Linnea Pullover pattern (page 85). It's your how-to guide. Don't miss it.

LINNEA PULLOVER

✳ ✳ ✳ INTERMEDIATE 1

This lovely floral pattern was inspired by the Scandinavian folk-art tradition known as rosemåling. The Linnea Pullover is knit top down, so the colorwork fun starts right away. It's fun to watch the pattern grow. While totally feasible for a beginner, this is the most complicated colorwork sweater in the book, making it a great place to learn the ins and outs of catching floats with both the main and contrasting colors. It's still not too hard. Just take the colorwork stitch by stitch, round by round. I suggest knitting the yoke in a quiet place without distraction. Take heart: Colorwork won't always take so much concentration. After the yoke, you can relax and finish the body and sleeves while chatting with family and friends. It's a joy to knit with a happy colorwork yoke smiling up at you, encouraging you to finish quickly because you really want to wear this sweater.

SKILLS YOU'LL PRACTICE

Long-tail cast on (page 184). Duplicate stitch join (page 183). Joining in the round seamlessly (page 37). Working 1x1 ribbing (k1, p1). Knitting with two colors in the round, left and right together (pages 41–42). Reading a chart (page 9). Catching floats with the main and contrasting colors (pages 85–87). Backward loop increase (page 182). Casting on stitches for the underarm. Picking up stitches for the sleeve (page 186). DPN work for the sleeves. Splicing yarn (page 186). Weaving a new yarn color in (and out) (pages 38–39 and 44–45). K2tog decrease (page 184). Ssk decrease (page 186).

SIZES

XXS (XS, S, SM, M, ML, L, XL, 2XL, 3XL, 4XL)

3 inches (7.5 cm) positive ease

MATERIALS

YARN: DK | Brooklyn Tweed Arbor | 100% American Targhee Wool | 145 yards (132 m) per 1.75-ounce (50-g) skein

MAIN COLOR (MC): Rainer (Blue) | 6 (6, 6, 7, 7, 7, 8, 8, 8, 9, 10) skeins [825 (840, 870, 945, 975, 1015, 1075, 1125, 1170, 1245, 1345) yards] / [754 (768, 795, 864, 891, 928, 982, 1028, 1069, 1138, 1229) m]

CONTRAST COLOR (CC): Hammock (White) | 1 (1, 1, 2, 2, 2, 2, 2, 2, 3, 3) skein(s) [145 (145, 145, 290, 290, 290, 290, 290, 290, 435, 490) yards] / [132 (132, 132, 265, 265, 265, 265, 265, 265, 397, 448) m]

NEEDLES: One 32-inch (80-cm) or 40-inch (100-cm) circular needle for the body and one set of double-pointed needles (DPNs), FlexiFlips, or a 16-inch (40-cm) circular needle for the sleeves in size needed to obtain gauge in colorwork and single color

SUGGESTED NEEDLE SIZE: US 7 (4.5 mm)

One 32-inch (80-cm) or 40-inch (100-cm) circular needle for the ribbing on the body, one 16-inch (40-cm) for the ribbing at the neck, and one set of double-pointed needles (DPNs) or FlexiFlips for the ribbing on the sleeves in three sizes smaller than gauge-size needles

SUGGESTED NEEDLE SIZE: US 4 (3.5 mm)

ADDITIONAL MATERIALS

Stitch marker, measuring tape, scissors, and tapestry needle

GAUGE AND SWATCH

19 stitches and 24 rounds = 4 inches (10 cm)

Please swatch in the round to determine needle size.

> **NOTE:** Swatch in both single color and in colorwork. You may need to knit the single-color part of the sweater with a smaller needle than the colorwork section. The gauge is the same throughout the sweater.

FINISHED MEASUREMENTS

CHEST: 30¼ (33¾, 36¼, 38¾, 41¼, 43¾, 46¼, 48¾, 52¼, 55½, 58) inches [77 (85.75, 92, 98.5, 104.75, 111, 117.5, 124, 132.75, 141, 147.5) cm]

BODY LENGTH TO UNDERARM: 13½ (14, 14, 15, 16, 16½, 17, 18, 19, 20, 21) inches [34 (35.5, 35.5, 38, 40.5, 42, 43, 45.75, 48, 50.75, 53.5) cm]

SLEEVE LENGTH: 17 (17½, 18, 18½, 19, 19½, 19½, 20, 20, 21, 21) inches [43 (44.5, 46, 47, 48, 49.5, 49.5, 50.5, 50.5, 53.5, 53.5) cm]

YOKE DEPTH: 8¾ (9, 9¼, 9⅓, 9½, 9¾, 10, 10¼, 10¾, 11½, 12) inches [22.25 (22.75, 23.5, 23.75, 24.25, 24.75, 25.5, 26.25, 27.5, 29.25, 30.5) cm]

TOTAL LENGTH: 22¼ (23, 23¼, 24⅓, 25½, 26¼, 27, 28¼, 29¾, 31½, 33) inches [56.5 (58.5, 59, 61.75, 64.75, 66.5, 68.5, 71.75, 75.5, 80, 84) cm]

INSTRUCTIONS

1. CAST ON NECKBAND STITCHES

With a smaller 16-inch (40-cm) needle and the MC, using a long-tail cast on, cast on 78 (84, 90, 96, 102, 108, 114, 120, 126, 132, 138) stitches.

2. NECKBAND RIBBING

Place a marker at the beginning of the round. Join, being careful not to twist the cast-on stitches. Row 1: *Knit 1, purl 1.* Repeat from * to * for 3 (3, 3, 3, 4, 4, 5, 5, 5, 5) rows. With the MC, knit one row.

3. KNIT YOKE

Now the fun starts. Switch to a gauge-size needle [US 7 (4.5 mm)]. The beginning of the round is located at the back-right shoulder (just after the back stitches and before the right-sleeve stitches). Begin colorwork. Carry the CC in your left hand and the MC in your right hand (making sure that the CC is in the dominant position). Begin knitting the chart (page 90) on Stitch 6 of Round 1. Catch the floats where necessary on Rounds 3, 7, 10, 13, 22, 26, 31, 32, 36, 37, 38, 42, 43, 44, and 47. Read the tutorial on pages 85–87 for tips. Knit Rounds 2–46. Repeat the chart from right to left 13 (14, 15, 16, 17, 18, 19, 20, 21, 22, 23) times on each round. Rounds 1, 2, 7, 10, 21, and 24 are increase rounds. Increase with a backward loop in the color indicated on the chart. Total stitches: 208 (224, 240, 256, 272, 288, 304, 320, 336, 352, 368). Finish knitting the chart to complete the yoke. Break the CC. Continuing with the MC, knit 3 (4, 5, 6, 7, 8, 9, 10, 13, 17, 20) rounds, or until you have reached 8¾ (9, 9¼, 9⅓, 9½, 9¾, 10, 10¼, 10¾, 11½, 12) inches [22 (22.5, 23, 23.5, 24, 24.5, 25, 26, 27.5, 29, 30) cm] or the desired depth of the yoke.

CATCHING FLOATS 101

GUIDELINES FOR CATCHING FLOATS

Weave in the color you are not knitting with whenever there are more than five consecutive stitches in a row of one color. (For finer gauge yarn, you can go up to eight stitches.) Just remember that you don't want a float to be longer than 1 inch (2.5 cm).

Generally, I catch the float in the center of the cluster of stitches of the same color. If there are five stitches in a row, I don't have to catch, but I usually opt to catch on the third stitch. If there are seven stitches in a row, I catch on the fourth. If there are eleven stitches in a row, I might catch on the fourth and eighth. You get the picture. There is flexibility here. I like to catch in the center so that the floats are the same length. But never catch a float in the exact same spot on two consecutive rows. If you do, the catch will show through on the right side of the knitting. And nobody wants that. But no worries, it's easy to stagger where you catch the floats.

Learn to catch floats with both the main color and the contrasting color.

CATCHING CONTRASTING COLOR FLOATS (A 2-STITCH PROCESS)

1.

Stitch one: Put the right needle into the first stitch as to knit and place the CC yarn over the right needle.

2.

Wrap the MC yarn counterclockwise around the right needle.

3.

Lift the CC off the right needle.

4.

Knit with the MC as usual.

5.

Stitch two: Insert the needle as to knit and wrap the MC over the needle. This catches the float.

6.

Complete the stitch.

CATCHING MAIN COLOR FLOATS (A 1-STITCH PROCESS)

1.

Insert the right needle as to knit.

2.

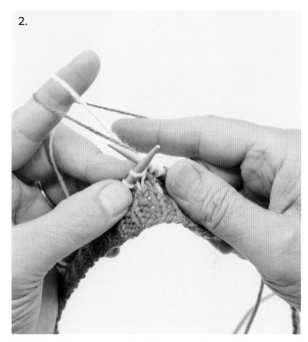

Throw the MC to the left of the CC on the left index finger.

3.

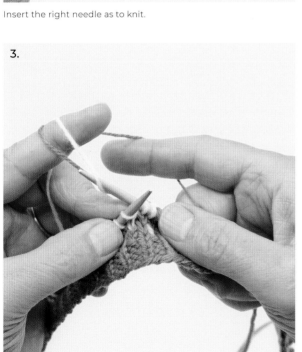

Knit with the CC.

4.

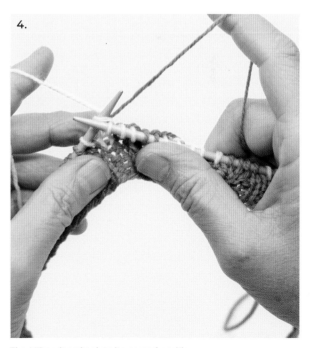

The MC springs back to its normal position.

working yarn between the two needles to the front and purl across the right-sleeve stitches and then across 64 (70, 76, 82, 88, 92, 98, 104, 110, 116, 122) back stitches and finally across the 40 (42, 44, 46, 48, 52, 54, 56, 58, 60, 62) left-sleeve stitches. Work a GSR in this manner: Turn and bring the yarn to the front of the work and, with the right needle, slip the first stitch off the left needle to the right needle. Tug on the working yarn and bring it over the right needle to the back. Knit one short row, stopping 3 stitches before the double stitch created by the GSR on the right sleeve. Work a GSR. Purl to 3 stitches before the double stitch created by the GSR on the left sleeve. Work a GSR. Knit one row, stopping 3 stitches before the double stitch created by the GSR. Work a GSR. Purl to 3 stitches before the double stitch. Work a GSR. Knit around until you reach the BOR marker. Knit one round while knitting all the double stitches together. Continue knitting until you reach the beginning of the round marker.

4. ADD OPTIONAL SHORT ROWS

Short rows improve the fit of the sweater by lowering the neckline in the front of the garment. To do this, work three German short rows on each side of the shoulder. With the MC, knit across the 40 (42, 44, 46, 48, 52, 54, 56, 58, 60, 62) right-sleeve stitches. Work a German short row (GSR) in this manner: Turn work. Bring your working yarn to the front and, with the tip of the right needle, slip the first stitch off the left needle to the right needle, tug the working yarn, and bring it over the top of the left needle, creating a double stitch. Bring the

5. DIVIDE YOKE AND KNIT BODY

Set aside stitches for the sleeves and knit the body. This round divides the yoke into the body and the sleeve stitches. Place 40 (42, 44, 46, 48, 52, 54, 56, 58, 60, 62) stitches on a holder for the right sleeve. Using a backward loop cast on, cast on 8 (10, 10, 10, 10, 12, 12, 12, 14, 16, 16) stitches for the right underarm. Knit across 64 (70, 76, 82, 88, 92, 98, 104, 110, 116, 122) stitches for the front. Place the next 40 (42, 44, 46, 48, 52, 54, 56, 58, 60, 62) stitches on a holder for the left sleeve. Using a backward-loop cast-on method, cast on 8 (10, 10, 10, 10, 12, 12, 12, 14, 16, 16) stitches for the left underarm. Knit across 64 (70, 76, 82, 88, 92, 98, 104, 110, 116, 122) back stitches. Total body stitches: 144 (160, 172, 184, 196, 208, 220, 232, 248, 264, 276).

Continue knitting in the round until the body measures 11½ (12, 12, 13, 14, 14½, 15, 16, 17, 18, 19) inches [29 (30.5, 30.5, 33, 35.5, 37, 38, 40.5, 43, 46, 48) cm] from the underarm or 2 inches (5 cm) shorter than the final length of the body. Try on your Linnea. You are going to want to tailor this measurement for the perfect fit for you. Adjust body to the desired measurement if needed. Switch to a US 4 (3.5 mm) circular needle and work 1x1 ribbing (k1, p1) in the round until the ribbing measures 2 inches (5 cm). Bind off all stitches loosely. Break yarn, leaving an 8-inch (20-cm) tail. Thread the tail of the yarn onto a tapestry needle. With a duplicate stitch, connect the last stitch of the round to the first stitch of the round.

6. KNIT LEFT SLEEVE

Transfer the 40 (42, 44, 46, 48, 52, 54, 56, 58, 60, 62) sleeve stitches onto a gauge-size 16-inch (40-cm) circular needle for the left sleeve. With the MC, pick up and knit 8 (10, 10, 10, 10, 12, 12, 12, 14, 16, 16) stitches for the underarm. Be careful and neatly pick up the stitches so that there aren't any holes between the arm stitches and the underarm stitches. (Hint: Leave a 10-inch [25.5-cm] tail to close up any holes if needed.) Place a marker in the middle of the underarm stitches to mark the beginning of the round. Total sleeve stitches: 48 (52, 54, 56, 58, 64, 66, 68, 72, 76, 78).

Knit in the round until the sleeve measures 2½ inches (6.5 cm). Work a decrease round in this manner: Knit around and stop 2 stitches before the marker at the beginning of the round. Ssk. Slip marker. Knit 1. K2tog = 2 decreased stitches. Continue knitting one decrease round every 2 (2, 2, 2, 2, 2, 1¼, 1¼, 1¼, 1¼, 1¼) inches [5 (5, 5, 5, 5, 5, 3, 3, 3, 3, 3) cm]. Continue decreasing a total of 4 (5, 5, 6, 6, 8, 8, 8, 9, 11, 11) decrease rounds until you have 40 (42, 44, 44, 46, 48, 50, 52, 54, 54, 56) stitches. Continue knitting until the sleeve measures 15 (15½, 16, 16½, 17, 17½, 17½, 18, 18, 19, 19) inches [38 (39.5, 40.5, 42, 43, 44.5, 44.5, 46, 46, 48, 48) cm] or 2 inches (5 cm) short of desired sleeve length from underarm to cuff.

Switch to smaller DPNs. Work 1x1 ribbing (k1, p1) for 2 inches (5 cm). Bind off all stitches. Break yarn, leaving an 8-inch (20-cm) tail. Thread the tail of the yarn onto a tapestry needle. With a duplicate stitch, connect the last stitch of the round to the first stitch of the round. Weave in the tail.

7. KNIT RIGHT SLEEVE

Repeat Step 6 and knit the right sleeve.

8. FINISHING

Weave in all the ends. Steam block. Congrats! You mastered catching floats with the MC and the CC while making a beautiful top-down sweater. Win/win!

LINNEA SCHEMATIC

A- Chest circumference: 30¼ (33¾, 36¼, 38¾, 41¼, 43¾, 46¼, 48¾, 52¼, 55½, 58) inches [77 (85.75, 92, 98.5, 104.75, 111, 117.5, 124, 132.75, 141, 147.5) cm]

B- Body length to underarm: 13½ (14, 14, 15, 16, 16½, 17, 18, 19, 20, 21) inches [34 (35.5, 35.5, 38, 40.5, 42, 43, 45.75, 48.25, 50.75, 53.5) cm]

C- Sleeve length: 17 (17½, 18, 18½, 19, 19½, 19½, 20, 20, 21, 21) inches [43 (44.5, 46, 47, 48, 49.5, 49.5, 50.5, 50.5, 53.5, 53.5) cm]

D- Yoke depth: 8¾ (9, 9¼, 9⅓, 9½, 9¾, 10, 10¼, 10¾, 11½, 12) inches [22.25 (22.75, 23.5, 23.75, 24.25, 24.75, 25.5, 26.25, 27.5, 29.25, 30.5) cm]

E- Total front length of sweater: 22¼ (23, 23¼, 24⅓, 25½, 26¼, 27, 28¼, 29¾, 31½, 33) inches [56.5 (58.5, 59, 61.75, 64.75, 66.5, 68.5, 71.75, 75.5, 80. 84) cm]

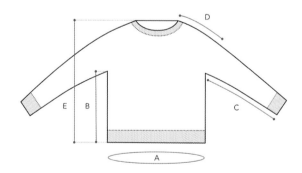

KEY

| x | = No stitch

| O | = Catch floats here

▲ = Increase one stitch with a backward loop

▢ = Contrasting Color (CC)

▨ = Main Color (MC)

LINNEA CHART

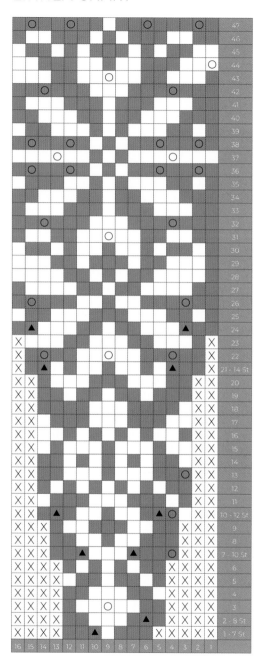

SETESDAL COWL

✸✸ ADVENTUROUS BEGINNER

In Norway, knitting is such a part of daily life that valleys, regions, and towns each have their own knitting tradition and style. The patterns from Setesdal have become a symbol of Norway around the world. Traditionally, the intense colorwork is located across the chest and shoulders and at the top of the sleeves. This cowl uses traditional XO (Kors og Kringle) patterns that are commonly found on sweaters from Setesdal. Row by row, the patterns are quite simple to knit and easy to memorize. Technically, you don't have to catch floats on this project, but there are a few places on Rounds 21 and 29 where there are five stitches of the main color in a row, so you can practice catching floats there if you like. Because cowls are worn to cover your neck and face, you will want to knit this cowl with the softest yarn possible so it feels dreamy next to your skin.

SKILLS YOU'LL PRACTICE

Long-tail cast on (page 184). Joining in the round seamlessly (page 37). Working 2x2 ribbing (k2, p2). Weaving a new yarn color in (and out) (pages 38–39 and 44–45). Knitting with two colors in the round, left and right together (pages 41–42). Reading a chart (page 9). Catching floats (pages 85–87). Backward loop increase (page 182). K2tog decrease (page 184). Binding off (page 182). Duplicate stitch join (page 183).

SIZE

One size fits most

MATERIALS

YARN: DK | Woolfolk Tov-DK | 100% Ovis 21 Ultimate Merino Wool | 160 yards (146 m) per 1.75-ounce (50-g) skein

MAIN COLOR (MC): DK 07 (Blue) | 1 skein [160 yards (146 m)]

CONTRASTING COLOR (CC): DK 02 (Light Grey) | 1 skein [100 yards (91 m)]

NEEDLES: One 24-inch (60-cm) circular needle in size needed to obtain gauge

SUGGESTED NEEDLE SIZE: US 5 (3.75 mm)

One 24-inch (60-cm) circular needle 2 sizes smaller than gauge-size needle

SUGGESTED NEEDLE SIZE: US 3 (3.25 mm)

ADDITIONAL MATERIALS

Stitch marker, scissors, and tapestry needle

GAUGE AND SWATCH

24 stitches and 28 rows = 4 inches (10 cm)

Worked in stranded colorwork with larger needles

FINISHED MEASUREMENTS

26½ x 9½ inches (67 x 24 cm)

INSTRUCTIONS

1. CAST ON

With smaller needles and the MC, using a long-tail cast on, cast on 156 stitches.

2. JOIN AND WORK 2X2 RIBBING

Join for working in the round, being careful not to twist the cast-on stitches. Round 1: Place marker at the beginning of the round. *Knit 2, purl 2.* Repeat from * to * all the way around. Work 2x2 ribbing for another eight rounds.

3. KNIT ROUND 1 OF CHART

Continuing with the MC, knit one round and increase 4 stitches evenly spaced with a backward loop. *Knit 39, then make one stitch.* Repeat from * to * four times. Total stitches: 160. During the last repeat, stop 5 stitches before the marker and weave in the CC so that you are ready to begin with both colors after the marker.

4. WORK COLORWORK

Slip marker. Change to larger needles for the colorwork portion and begin working the chart (page 94) on Stitch 1 of Round 2. Read the chart from right to left. Repeat the chart 10 times for a total of 160 stitches. Knit Rounds 2–51 of the chart. Follow the chart carefully on the first colorwork round to establish the pattern. Carry the CC in your left hand and the MC in your right hand. This will ensure that the pattern yarn is in the dominant position.

If you are carrying the yarn in one hand, carry the CC to the left of the MC. Whichever method you use to knit with two colors, be consistent throughout the entire cowl. On Rounds 21 and 29: Catch the floats of the CC whenever there are five or more consecutive stitches of the same color in a row. Finish knitting the chart and then break the CC, leaving a 6-inch (15.25 cm) tail.

5. KNIT ONE ROUND AND WEAVE OUT THE TAIL FROM THE CONTRASTING COLOR

With the MC only, knit one round. Weave out the tail from the CC. Decrease 4 stitches evenly spaced by knitting 2 stitches together. *Knit 38 stitches, then k2tog.* Repeat from * to * four times. Total stitches: 156.

6. WORK 2X2 RIBBING

Switch to smaller needles. Continuing with the MC only, work 2x2 ribbing (k2, p2) for eight rounds.

7. BIND OFF ALL STITCHES

Bind off with the following pattern: *k2, p2, k2, p2tog.* This may seem tricky, but all you do is bind off following the established ribbing pattern for the first 6 stitches (k2, p2, k2), then purl 2 stitches together while continuing to bind off. Repeat from * to * 19 times, all the way around. End with k2, p2. Break yarn, leaving an 8-inch (20-cm) tail. Thread the tail of the yarn onto a tapestry needle. With a duplicate stitch, connect the last stitch of the bind-off round to the first stitch of the bind-off round.

8. FINISHING

Weave in all the ends, steam block your cowl, and wear or gift right away.

SETESDAL COWL SCHEMATIC

A- Circumference: 26½ inches (67 cm)

B- Height: 9½ inches (24 cm)

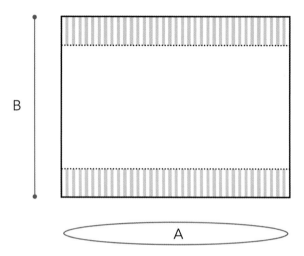

KEY

■ = Contrasting Color (CC)

■ = Main Color (MC)

SETESDAL CHART

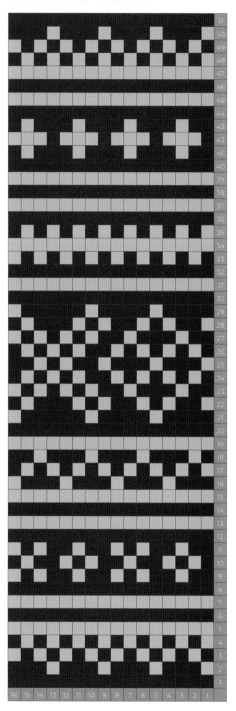

DAGNA HAT

✻✻ ADVENTUROUS BEGINNER

The Dagna Hat was inspired by my grandpa's sister, my aunt Dag, who was a child in Norway and a teenager in America. Our family had a fabulous photo of her in a Norwegian sweater. The story I heard every time I saw that photo was that Dagna could out ski the boys. I decided to make the Dagna Hat with an American yarn, just like my immigrant ancestors made Norwegian things with American products. I chose Harrisville Designs' rich and subtle Nightshades and Daylights. It's black-and-white yarn marbled with blue. Dagna is knit in the round, bottom up. The colorwork is super easy and a good place to learn how to catch floats. This hat can be made for women or men, and as a traditional or slouchy beanie. Wear it as-is or add a snap-on, faux fur pom-pom just for fun.

SKILLS YOU'LL PRACTICE

Long-tail cast on (page 184). Joining in the round seamlessly (page 37). Working 2x2 ribbing (k2, p2). Weaving a new yarn color in (and out) (pages 38–39 and 44–45). Knitting with two colors in the round, left and right together (pages 41–42). Reading a chart (page 9). Catching floats (pages 85–87). Backward loop increase (page 182). K2tog decrease (page 184). Ssk decrease (page 186).

SIZES

Adult S (M, L) with two length options. The first option is for a traditional fit. The second is for a slouchier hat. The medium size fits an average-size head [22–24 inches (56–61 cm) around]. The gauge changes depending on the desired size of the hat. Sample hat is a medium worked with the traditional length.

MATERIALS

YARN: MAIN COLOR (MC): DK | Harrisville Designs Nightshades DK 3-ply | American Cormo and Wool | 250 yards (228 m) per 3.5-ounce (100-g) skein | 1 skein [90 yards (83 m)] | Color: Last Call (Navy)

CONTRASTING COLOR (CC): DK | Harrisville Designs Daylights DK 3-ply | American Cormo and Wool | 250 yards (228 m) per 3.5-ounce (100-g) skein | 1 skein [35 yards (32 m)] | Color: Chirp

TOTAL YARDAGE FOR HAT: approximately 125 yards (115 m)

NEEDLES: One 16-inch (40-cm) circular needle and one pair of double-pointed needles (DPNs) as needed to obtain gauge in both colorwork and single color for the body and crown of the hat

SUGGESTED NEEDLE SIZE: US 5 (6, 7) [3.75 (4, 4.5) mm]

One 16-inch (40-cm) circular needle two sizes smaller than gauge-size needle for the brim

SUGGESTED NEEDLE SIZE: US 3 (4, 5) [3.25 (3.5, 3.75) mm]

ADDITIONAL MATERIALS

Stitch markers, tapestry needle, scissors, and measuring tape

GAUGE AND SWATCH

The size of the hat is determined by the gauge. The stitch count is the same in all sizes. Please swatch in stranded colorwork and in single color to establish the gauge. Adjust needle size if necessary when changing from colorwork to knitting with a single color.

THE GAUGE FOR AN ADULT SMALL HAT:
22 stitches and 25 rounds = 4 inches (10 cm)

THE GAUGE FOR AN ADULT MEDIUM HAT:
20 stitches and 24 rounds = 4 inches (10 cm)

THE GAUGE FOR AN ADULT LARGE HAT:
18 stitches and 22 rounds = 4 inches (10 cm)

FINISHED MEASUREMENTS

Circumference: 17½ (19¼, 21¼) inches [44.5 (49, 54) cm]

Length:

Traditional fit: 10 (10, 10½) inches [25.25 (25.25, 26.75) cm]

Slouchy option: 11 (11, 11½) inches [28 (28, 29.25) cm]

INSTRUCTIONS

1. CAST ON BRIM

With smaller needle and MC, using a long-tail cast on, cast on 96 stitches.

2. JOIN AND KNIT RIBBING

Join for working in the round, being careful not to twist the cast-on stitches. Place a marker at the beginning of the round. Round 1: *K2, p2.* Repeat from * to *. (Hint: Work the first 2 stitches with the working yarn, and with the tail from the long-tail, cast on for a seamless join.) Make sure on the next round to treat the first 2 stitches after the join as 2 stitches (not 4) by knitting the working yarn and the tail together as one stitch. Work 2x2 ribbing for 3½ (3½, 3¾) inches [9 (9, 9.5) cm] for a traditional hat or 4½ (4½, 4¾) inches [11.5 (11.5, 12) cm] for a slouchier hat. Total stitches: 96.

3. BEGIN COLORWORK

With the MC, knit one round and increase 2 stitches evenly spaced with a backward loop. Total stitches: 98. Work the chart (page 99) from right to left, beginning with Stitch 1 of Round 1. Repeat the chart seven times. Catch the floats on Rounds 5, 8, 10, and 13. I like to catch the floats whenever there are five or more consecutive stitches of the same color in a row. Keep the CC in the dominant position.

When knitting with one color in each hand, hold the CC in the left hand and the MC in the right. If you are knitting with both colors in one hand, then place the CC to the left of the MC. Be consistent throughout the entire hat. When knitting with one color, knit with whichever hand you are the most comfortable with. Continue knitting Rounds 1–16 of the chart. On Round 17, decrease 2 stitches by knitting 2 stitches together twice, evenly spaced. Total stitches: 96. Continuing with the MC only, knit until the hat measures 8 (8, 8½) inches [20.5 (20.5, 21.5) cm] or 9 (9, 9½) inches [23 (23, 24) cm] from cast-on edge.

4. BEGIN DECREASING FOR CROWN

Continue with the MC and decrease every round as follows.

ROUND 1: *Ssk, knit 20 stitches, k2tog.* Repeat from * to * four times. Total stitches: 88.

ROUND 2: *Ssk, knit 18 stitches, k2tog.* Repeat from * to * four times. Total stitches: 80.

ROUND 3: *Ssk, knit 16 stitches, k2tog.* Repeat from * to * four times. Total stitches: 72.

ROUND 4: *Ssk, knit 14 stitches, k2tog.* Repeat from * to * four times. Total stitches: 64.

ROUND 5: *Ssk, knit 12 stitches, k2tog.* Repeat from * to * four times. Total stitches: 56.

ROUND 6: *Ssk, knit 10 stitches, k2tog.* Repeat from * to * four times. Total stitches: 48.

ROUND 7: *Ssk, knit 8 stitches, k2tog.* Repeat from * to * four times. Total stitches: 40.

ROUND 8: *Ssk, knit 6 stitches, k2tog.* Repeat from * to * four times. Total stitches: 32.

ROUND 9: *Ssk, knit 4 stitches, k2tog.* Repeat from * to * four times. Total stitches: 24.

ROUND 10: *Ssk, knit 2 stitches, k2tog.* Repeat from * to * four times. Total stitches: 16.

ROUND 11: *Ssk, k2tog.* Repeat from * to * four times. Total stitches: 8.

ROUND 12: Knit one round.

Final stitch count is 8 stitches. Break yarn, leaving a 6-inch (15.25-cm) tail. Thread the tail of the yarn onto a tapestry needle and through the remaining 8 live stitches and pull to close the crown. Put the needle through the hole at the top of the hat. Pull to gather again. Weave in tail.

5. FINISHING

Weave in all the ends. Steam block and wear. You have enough yarn left for two more hats (if you switch your MC and CC). Happy winter!

DAGNA SCHEMATIC

A- Circumference: 17½ (19¼, 21¼) inches [44.5 (49, 54) cm]

B- Length: 10 (10, 10½) inches [25.25 (25.25, 26.75) cm]

Slouchy option: 11 (11, 11½) inches [28 (28, 29.25) cm]

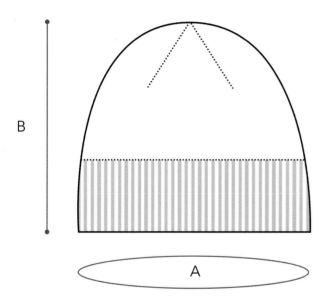

DAGNA CHART

KEY

☐ = Contrasting Color (CC)

▨ = Main Color (MC)

EVA JUMPER

✱✱✱ INTERMEDIATE 1

The Eva Jumper was inspired by the short-sleeved jumpers of the 1940s. Eva is a four-season jumper with short sleeves and a classic feel. Is it vintage or is it modern? Who can tell? It's fun to make and wear sweaters like this one that feel timeless. The yoke is a geometric tulip motif with long stems and lots of leaves. You may choose to knit Eva in the spring or summer. But it's also fun to knit in the winter when you are dreaming of spring. It's knit from the bottom up and—as with the Magnus Pullover (page 63) and Maja Pullover (page 69)—the Eva Jumper makes a great beginner sweater. The pattern is repetitive in a good way, and the short sleeves make it a quicker knit overall. The only difference in difficulty between this jumper and the sweaters in the previous chapter is that here you will need to catch floats between the stems of the tulips.

SKILLS YOU'LL PRACTICE

Long-tail cast on (page 184). Duplicate stitch join (page 183). Joining in the round seamlessly (page 37). Working 2x2 ribbing (k2, p2). DPN work for the sleeves. Backward loop increase (page 182). Splicing yarn (page 186). Joining body and sleeves onto one needle. Weaving a new yarn color in (and out) (pages 38–39 and 44–45). Knitting with two colors in the round, left and right together (pages 41–42). Reading a chart (page 9). Catching floats (pages 85–87). K2tog decrease (page 184). Ssk decrease (page 186). Mattress stitch (page 185).

SIZES

XXS (XS, S, SM, M, ML, L, XL, 2XL, 3XL, 4XL)

3 inches (7.5 cm) positive ease

MATERIALS

YARN: DK | Brooklyn Tweed Arbor | 100% American Targhee Wool | 145 yards (139 m) per 1.75-ounce (50-g) skein

MAIN COLOR (MC): Seaglass (Blue/Green) | 5 (5, 5, 6, 6, 6, 7, 7, 7, 8, 9) skeins [680 (700, 725, 780, 830, 870, 930, 980, 1025, 1100, 1200) yards] / [621 (640, 663, 713, 759, 796, 850, 896, 937, 1106, 1097) m]

CONTRASTING COLOR (CC): Hammock (White) | 1 (1, 1, 2, 2, 2, 2, 2, 3, 3, 3) skein(s) [100 (120, 140, 190, 220, 240, 260, 290, 320, 380, 410) yards] / [91 (110, 128, 174, 201, 219, 239, 265, 293, 347, 375) m]

NEEDLES: One 32-inch (80-cm) or 40-inch (100-cm) circular needle for the body and one set of double-pointed needles (DPNs), FlexiFlips, or a 16-inch (40-cm) circular needle for the sleeves in size needed to obtain gauge

SUGGESTED NEEDLE SIZE: US 7 (4.5 mm)

(Materials continued)

One 32-inch (80-cm) or 40-inch (100-cm) circular needle for the body ribbing and one set of double-pointed needles (DPNs), FlexiFlips, or a 16-inch (40-cm) circular needle for the ribbing on the sleeves that is three sizes smaller than gauge-size needles

SUGGESTED NEEDLE SIZE: US 4 (3.5 mm)

ADDITIONAL MATERIALS

Tapestry needle, stitch markers, scissors, and measuring tape

GAUGE AND SWATCH

19 stitches and 24 rounds = 4 inches (10 cm)

Please swatch in the round to determine needle size.

> **NOTE:** Swatch in both single color and in colorwork. You may need to knit the single-color part of the sweater with a smaller needle than the colorwork section. The gauge is the same throughout the sweater.

FINISHED MEASUREMENTS

CHEST: 30¼ (33¾, 36¼, 38¾, 41¼, 43¾, 46¼, 48¾, 52¼, 55½, 58) inches [77 (86, 92, 98.5, 104.75, 111, 117.5, 124, 132.75, 141, 147.5) cm]

BODY LENGTH TO UNDERARM: 12½ (13, 13½, 14, 14½, 15, 15½, 15½, 16, 16, 16) inches [32 (33, 34.5, 35.5, 37, 38, 39.5, 39.5, 40.5, 40.5, 40.5) cm]

SLEEVE LENGTH: 3½ (3½, 3¾, 3¾, 3¾, 4¼, 4¼, 4¼, 4¾, 4¾, 4¾) inches [9 (9, 9.5, 9.5, 9.5, 10.75, 10.75, 10.75, 12, 12, 12) cm]

YOKE DEPTH: 8¾ (8¾, 9, 9, 9¼, 9¼, 9¼, 9¼, 9½, 9½, 9½) inches [22.5 (22.5, 23, 23, 23.5, 23.5, 23.5, 23.5, 24, 24, 24) cm]

TOTAL LENGTH: 21¼ (21¾, 22½, 23, 23¾, 24¼, 24¾, 24¾, 25½, 25½, 25½) inches [54 (55.25, 57, 58.5, 60.5, 61.5, 63, 63, 64.75, 64.75, 64.75) cm]

INSTRUCTIONS

1. CAST ON

With smaller needles, and MC, using a long-tail cast on, cast on 144 (160, 172, 184, 196, 208, 220, 232, 248, 264, 276) stitches.

2. RIBBING

Place a marker at the beginning of the round. Join for knitting in the round, being careful not to twist the stitches. Round 1: *K2, p2.* Repeat from * to * to the end of the round. (Hint: Work the first 2 stitches with the working yarn and the tail from the long-tail cast on for a seamless join.) Work 2x2 ribbing for another thirteen rounds.

3. KNIT BODY

Change to larger needles and continue knitting in the round until the body measures 12½ (13, 13½, 14, 14½, 15, 15½, 15½, 16, 16, 16) inches [32 (33, 34.5, 35.5, 37, 38, 39.5, 39.5, 40.5, 40.5, 40.5) cm] or until the desired length from the bottom of the sweater to the underarm. This is a tricky measurement because this sweater is cropped. Please measure from your underarm to where you want this sweater to hit you at your hips/waist. You are going to want to tailor this measurement for the perfect fit for you. When you have reached the perfect measurement for you, stop 4 (5, 5, 5, 5, 6, 6, 6, 7, 8, 8) stitches before the marker. Bind off the next 8 (10, 10, 10, 10, 12, 12, 12, 14, 16, 16) stitches for the underarm.

4. KNIT SLEEVE

With smaller FlexiFlips or a 16-inch (40-cm) circular needle and the MC, cast on 48 (52, 52, 56, 56, 64, 64, 68, 72, 76, 76) stitches. Place a marker and join by knitting from the last cast-on stitch to the first cast-on stitch. Work in 2x2 ribbing (k2, p2) for 12 (12, 12, 12, 12, 14, 14, 14, 14, 14, 14) rounds.

For sizes S, M, L, and 4XL, knit one round and increase 2 stitches evenly spaced for a total of 48 (52, 54, 56, 58, 64, 66, 68, 72, 76, 78) stitches.

CHANGE TO LARGER NEEDLES. Knit for 9 (9, 10, 10, 10, 12, 12, 12, 14, 14, 14) rounds. On the last round, stop knitting 4 (5, 5, 5, 5, 6, 6, 6, 7, 8, 8) stitches before the marker. Bind off the next 8 (10, 10, 10, 10, 12, 12, 12, 14, 16, 16) stitches.

5. JOIN SLEEVE TO THE BODY

Match up the stitches set aside for the underarm on the body to the stitches set aside for the underarm on the sleeve. Place a marker. Continuing with the yarn that was used for knitting the body, knit the left sleeve for 40 (42, 44, 46, 48, 52, 54, 56, 58, 60, 62) stitches. Knit across the front of the body for 64 (70, 76, 82, 88, 92, 98, 104, 110, 116, 122) stitches. Bind off the next 8 (10, 10, 10, 10, 12, 12, 12, 14, 16, 16) stitches for the second underarm. Now you are all ready to attach the second sleeve. Set work aside.

6. KNIT SECOND SLEEVE

Repeat Step 4 and knit the right sleeve.

7. JOIN SECOND SLEEVE TO THE BODY

Match up the stitches for the right underarm to the body. Knit from the front stitches to the right sleeve for 40 (42, 44, 46, 48, 52, 54, 56, 58, 60, 62) stitches. Continue knitting across the 64 (70, 76, 82, 88, 92, 98, 104, 110, 116, 122) stitches for the back of the jumper. You have joined the sleeves to the body and are ready to knit the yoke. Total stitches: 208 (224, 240, 256, 272, 288, 304, 320, 336, 352, 368). Knit 14 (14, 15, 15, 16, 16, 17, 17, 18, 18, 18) rounds.

NOTE: The marker is placed at the beginning of the round and is located at the back of the left shoulder of the sweater.

8. ADD OPTIONAL SHORT ROWS

Short rows improve the fit of the sweater by lowering the neckline in the front of the garment. Work three German short rows on each side of the shoulder. With the MC, knit across the 40 (42, 44, 46, 48, 52, 54, 56, 58, 60, 62) left-sleeve stitches. Work a German short row (GSR) in this manner: Turn work. Bring your working yarn to the front and, with the tip of the right needle, slip the first stitch off the left needle to the right needle, tug the working yarn and bring it over the top of the left needle, creating a double stitch. Bring the working yarn between the two needles to the front and purl across the sleeve stitches to the marker and then purl across 64 (70, 76, 82, 88, 92, 98, 104, 110, 116, 122) back stitches and across the 40 (42, 44, 46, 48, 52, 54, 56, 58, 60, 62) right-sleeve stitches. Turn and bring the yarn to the front of the work and, with the right needle, slip the first stitch from the left needle to the right needle. Tug the working yarn and bring it over the right needle to the back. Knit one short row, stopping 3 stitches before the double stitch created by the GSR. Work a GSR. Purl to 3 stitches before the double stitch. Work a GSR. Knit one short row, stopping 3 stitches before the double stitch created by the GSR. Work a GSR. Purl to 3 stitches before the double stitch. Work a GSR. Knit to the beginning of the round. Knit one round and knit all the double stitches together as you come to them and then knit to the end of the round.

9. KNIT THE YOKE

Now the fun starts. Carry the CC in your left hand and the MC in your right hand (making sure that the contrasting color is in the dominant position). Work the chart (page 105) beginning on Stitch 1 of Round 1. Repeat the chart 26 (28, 30, 32, 34, 36, 38, 40, 42, 44, 46) times. Rounds 22, 24, 30, 33, and 37 are decrease rounds. Decrease by knitting the 2 stitches marked with dots together as follows on each decrease round. Round 22: K2tog. Round 24: K2tog. Round 30: K2tog. Round 33: Ssk. Round 37: K2tog. Don't forget to stagger where you catch the floats on this sweater from round to round, or you will have a noticeable line where you caught the floats.

10. WORK NECKBAND

There are 78 (84, 90, 96, 102, 108, 114, 120, 126, 132, 138) stitches. With the MC, knit one round and adjust the stitch count as noted for each size by knitting 2 stitches together, evenly spaced 2 (0, 2, 0, 2, 0, 2, 0, 2, 0, 2) times. Total stitches: 76 (84, 88, 96, 100, 108, 112, 120, 124, 132, 136). Work 2x2 ribbing (k2, p2) for five rounds. Bind off all stitches working a k2, p2, k2, p2, k2, p2tog bind off all the way around 6 (7, 7, 8, 8, 9, 9, 10, 10, 11, 11) times and then continue to work in 2x2 ribbing to the end of the round as needed. Break yarn, leaving an 8-inch (20-cm) tail. Thread the tail of the yarn onto a tapestry needle. With a duplicate stitch, connect the last stitch of the round to the first stitch of the round.

11. FINISHING

Weave in all the ends and sew the underarm stitches together. (I like to do this with a duplicate stitch.) Steam block. Congrats! Your vintage jumper is ready to wear.

EVA SCHEMATIC

A- Chest circumference: 30¼ (33¾, 36¼, 38¾, 41¼, 43¾, 46¼, 48¾, 52¼, 55½, 58) inches [77 (86, 92, 98.5, 104.75, 111, 117.5, 124, 132.75, 141, 147.5) cm]

B- Body length to underarm: 12½ (13, 13½, 14, 14½, 15, 15½, 15½, 16, 16, 16) inches [32 (33, 34.5, 35.5, 37, 38, 39.5, 39.5, 40.5, 40.5, 40.5) cm]

C- Sleeve length: 3½ (3½, 3¾, 3¾, 3¾, 4¼, 4¼, 4¼, 4¾, 4¾, 4¾) inches [9 (9, 9.5, 9.5, 9.5, 10.75, 10.75, 10.75, 12, 12, 12) cm]

D- Yoke depth: 8¾ (8¾, 9, 9, 9¼, 9¼, 9¼, 9¼, 9½, 9½, 9½) inches [22.5 (22.5, 23, 23, 23.5, 23.5, 23.5, 23.5, 24, 24, 24) cm]

E- Total length: 21¼ (21¾, 22½, 23, 23¾, 24¼, 24¾, 24¾, 25½, 25½, 25½) inches [54 (55.25, 57, 58.5, 60.5, 61.5, 63, 63, 64.75, 64.75, 64.75) cm]

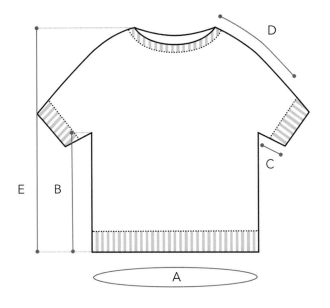

EVA CHART

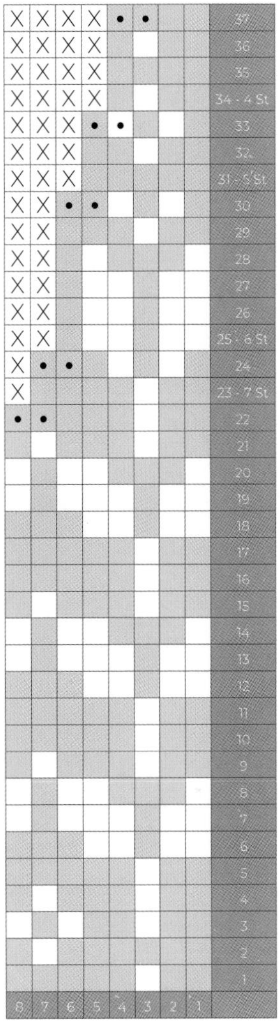

X	X	X	X	•	•			37
X	X	X	X					36
X	X	X	X					35
X	X	X	X					34 - 4 St
X	X	X	•	•				33
X	X	X						32
X	X	X						31 - 5 St
X	X	•	•					30
X	X							29
X	X							28
X	X							27
X	X							26
X	X							25 - 6 St
X	•	•						24
X								23 - 7 St
•	•							22
								21
								20
								19
								18
								17
								16
								15
								14
								13
								12
								11
								10
								9
								8
								7
								6
								5
								4
								3
								2
								1
8	7	6	5	4	3	2	1	

KEY

x	= No stitch
•	= Decrease by knitting the two dots together
☐	= Contrasting Color (CC)
▨	= Main Color (MC)

GRETA PULLOVER

✻ ✻ ✻ INTERMEDIATE 1

In Sweden, Midsommar celebrations are second only to Christmas on the festivity list. It's no surprise, really, in a land where winters are long and dark, that the arrival of summer and light is a major cause for celebration. I originally designed this happy sweater as a children's pattern (see the Little Greta Pullover, page 113). But the moment little 5-year-old Gracie tried on the prototype, every adult in the room was jealous and wanted one as well. The relaxed fit of Greta plays nicely with the cheery Midsommar yoke. It's knit in the round, bottom up, so the colorwork comes last like a reward. There are four colors in this sweater's flower-packed yoke, but don't freak out. I show you how to accomplish them by knitting only two colors at once and adding more colors with a duplicate stitch. This is a great trick. No one will ever know you didn't knit four colors at once.

SKILLS YOU'LL PRACTICE

Long-tail cast on (page 184). Duplicate stitch join (page 183). Joining in the round seamlessly (page 37). Working 1x1 ribbing (k1, p1). DPN work for the sleeves. Backward loop increase (page 182). Splicing yarn (page 186). Joining body and sleeves onto one needle. Weaving a new yarn color in (and out) (pages 38–39 and 44–45). Knitting with two colors in the round, left and right together (pages 41–42). Reading a chart (page 9). Catching floats (pages 85–87). K2tog decrease (page 184). Ssk decrease (page 186). Kitchener stitch (page 183). Duplicate stitch (page 183).

SIZES

XS (S, M, L, XL, 2XL, 3XL, 4XL)

3–5 inches (7.5–12.5 cm) positive ease

MATERIALS

YARN: Aran | Biches & Bûches Le Gros Lambswool | 100% Scottish Lambswool | 210 yards (192 m) per 3.5-ounce (100-g) skein

MAIN COLOR (MC): Undyed Off-White | 4 (5, 5, 5, 6, 6, 7, 7) skeins [800 (850, 900, 1000, 1100, 1200, 1300, 1400) yards] / [732 (777, 823, 914, 1006, 1097, 1189, 1280) m]

CONTRASTING COLOR 1 (CC1): Medium Blue | 1 skein [45 (49, 53, 56, 60, 65, 68, 70) yards] / [41 (45, 48, 51, 55, 59, 62, 64) m]

CONTRASTING COLOR 2 (CC2): Medium Red | 1 skein [34 (38, 40, 42, 46, 48, 50, 52) yards] / [31 (35, 37, 38, 42, 44, 46, 48) m]

CONTRASTING COLOR 3 (CC3): Dark Yellow | 1 skein [18 (19, 20, 21, 23, 24, 25, 25) yards] / [16 (17, 18, 19, 21, 22, 23, 23) m]

NEEDLES: One 32-inch (80-cm) or 40-inch (100-cm) circular needle for the body and one set of double-pointed needles (DPNs), FlexiFlips, or a 16-inch (40-cm) circular needle for the sleeves in size needed to obtain gauge in colorwork and single color

SUGGESTED NEEDLE SIZE: US 7 (4.5 mm)

One 32-inch (80-cm) or 40-inch (100-cm) circular needle for the body ribbing and one set of double-pointed needles (DPNs), FlexiFlips, or a 16-inch (40-cm) circular needle for the ribbing on the sleeves one size smaller than gauge-size needle

SUGGESTED NEEDLE SIZE: US 6 (4 mm)

ADDITIONAL MATERIALS

Tapestry needle, stitch markers, scissors, and measuring tape

GAUGE AND SWATCH

16 stitches and 19 rounds = 4 inches (10 cm)

Please swatch in the round to determine needle size.

> **NOTE:** Swatch in both one color and in colorwork. You may need to knit the single-color part of the sweater with a smaller needle than the colorwork section. The gauge is the same throughout the sweater.

FINISHED MEASUREMENTS

CHEST: 35 (40, 43, 46, 49, 52, 54, 56) inches [89 (101.5, 109.5, 117, 124.5, 132, 137, 142.5) cm]

BODY LENGTH TO UNDERARM: 15 (16, 16½, 17, 18, 19, 20, 20) inches [38 (40.5, 42, 43, 46, 48.5, 51, 51) cm]

SLEEVE LENGTH: 17 (18, 19, 19½, 20, 21, 21, 21) inches [43 (46, 48.5, 49.5, 51, 53.5, 53.5, 53.5) cm]

YOKE DEPTH: 8¼ (9½, 9¾, 9¾, 10½, 10¾, 11, 11¼) inches [21 (24, 24.75, 24.75, 26.75, 27.5, 28, 28.5) cm]

TOTAL LENGTH: 23¼ (25½, 26¼, 26¾, 28½, 29¾, 31, 31¼) inches [59 (64.75, 66.5, 68, 72.5, 75.5, 78.75, 79.5) cm]

INSTRUCTIONS

1. CAST ON

With smaller needles and the MC, using a long-tail cast on, cast on 140 (160, 172, 184, 196, 208, 216, 224) stitches.

2. RIBBING

Place a marker at the beginning of the round. Join for knitting in the round, being careful not to twist the cast-on stitches. Round 1: *Knit 1, purl 1.* Repeat from * to * all the way around. (Hint: Work the first 2 stitches with the working yarn and the tail from the long-tail cast on for a seamless join.) Work 1x1 ribbing for another 14 (14, 14, 14, 14, 16, 16, 16) rounds.

3. KNIT BODY

Change to larger needles. Knit in the round until the body measures 15 (16, 16½, 17, 18, 19, 20, 20) inches [38 (40.5, 42, 43, 45.5, 48.5, 51, 51) cm] or until the desired length to the underarm. Stop 4 (4, 5, 5, 5, 5, 6, 6) stitches before the marker. Place the next 8 (8, 9, 10, 10, 10, 11, 11) stitches on a holder for the underarm.

4. KNIT SLEEVE

With smaller DPNs and the MC, cast on 38 (40, 44, 44, 46, 48, 48, 50) stitches. Divide the stitches evenly between three DPNs. Place a marker and join (by knitting from the last cast-on stitch to the first cast-on stitch). Work in 1x1 ribbing for sixteen rounds.

Next round, change to larger needles and knit in the round until the sleeve measures 4 inches (10 cm). Increase one stitch right after the first stitch and before the last stitch of the round with a backward loop. Total stitches: 40 (42, 46, 46, 48, 50, 50, 52). For all sizes, increase 2 stitches in the same manner every 2 inches (5 cm) 4 (4, 4, 5, 6, 5, 7, 8) more times. Total sleeve stitches: 48 (50, 54, 56, 60, 60, 64, 68). Continue knitting until the sleeve measures 17 (18, 19, 19½, 20, 21, 21, 21) inches [43 (45.5, 48.5, 49.5, 51, 53.5, 53.5, 53.5) cm] or the desired length. On the last round, stop knitting 4 (4, 5, 5, 5, 5, 6, 6) stitches before the marker. Place the next 8 (8, 9, 10, 10, 10, 11, 11) stitches onto a holder for the underarm.

5. JOIN THE BODY TO THE FIRST SLEEVE FOR THE YOKE

Match up the stitches set aside for the underarm on the body to the stitches set aside for the underarm on the sleeve. Place a marker. Continuing with the yarn that was used for knitting the body, knit the left sleeve for 40 (42, 45, 46, 50, 50, 53, 57) stitches. Knit across the front of the body for 62 (72, 77, 82, 88, 94, 97, 101) stitches. Place the next 8 (8, 9, 10, 10, 10, 11, 11) stitches onto a holder for the second underarm. Now you are all ready to attach the second sleeve. Set work aside.

Knit one round, and for sizes M, L, and 4XL, adjust the stitches as follows: Knit one round and decrease 4 stitches by knitting the 2 stitches together where the body meets the sleeve. Total stitches: 204 (228, 240, 252, 276, 288, 300, 312). Continue to knit 2 (4, 5, 5, 6, 7, 8, 9) rounds.

> **NOTE:** The marker is placed at the beginning of the round and is located at the back of the left shoulder of the sweater.

8. KNIT THE YOKE

Now the fun starts. Work Chart 1 (2, 2, 2, 3, 3, 3, 3) (page 112) carrying the CC in your left hand and the MC in your right hand (making sure that the contrasting color is in the dominant position). Begin knitting the chart on the right bottom corner. Repeat the chart 17 (19, 20, 21, 23, 24, 25, 26) times in the round. Work only two colors at once per round. Work the stitch for the third color (marked with an X on the chart) with the MC and add the appropriate color later with a duplicate stitch.

Continue following the chart. Work decreases as indicated on the chart by knitting the stitches with dots together. The first decrease on each round is worked with a k2tog, and the second decrease on the round is worked with a ssk. Complete the chart. Total stitches: 68 (76, 80, 84, 92, 96, 100, 104).

> **NOTE:** If you are up to it, you can knit with three colors at once. Carry two in the left hand and one in the right hand.

6. KNIT THE SECOND SLEEVE

Repeat Step 4 and knit the right sleeve.

7. JOIN THE SECOND SLEEVE TO THE BODY

Match up the stitches for the right underarm to the body. Knit from the front stitches to the 40 (42, 45, 46, 50, 50, 53, 57) right-sleeve stitches. Continue knitting across the 62 (72, 77, 82, 88, 94, 97, 101) back stitches to the marker. Ta-da. You have joined the sleeves to the body and are ready to knit the yoke.

9. WORK NECKBAND

Switch to smaller needles and knit one row with the MC. Work 1x1 ribbing (k1, p1) for 7 (8, 8, 8, 9, 9, 10, 10) rounds. Bind off all stitches following the established ribbing pattern. While binding off, decrease 4 stitches evenly spaced around the neck by working a purl and a knit stitch together with a k2tog. Break yarn, leaving an 8-inch (20-cm) tail. Thread the tail of the yarn onto a tapestry needle. With a duplicate stitch, connect the last stitch of the round to the first stitch of the round.

10. FINISHING

With the appropriate color yarn and a tapestry needle, duplicate stitch the stitches marked with an X on the chart on top of the MC used to knit the stitch. (See duplicate stitch embroidery on page 55.) When adding a color, work all the way around the yoke on the same round as if you are knitting with that color, weaving in the strand of yarn with the tapestry needle to catch the floats, and at the end of the round to secure.

Weave in all the ends and graft together the underarm stitches, using the Kitchener Stitch. Steam block. Congrats! Wear or gift right away.

GRETA SCHEMATIC

A- Chest circumference: 35 (40, 43, 46, 49, 52, 54, 56) inches [89 (101.5, 109.5, 117, 124.5, 132, 137, 142.5) cm]

B- Body length to underarm: 15 (16, 16½, 17, 18, 19, 20, 20) inches [38 (40.5, 42, 43, 45.5, 48.5, 51, 51) cm]

C- Sleeve length: 17 (18, 19, 19½, 20, 21, 21, 21) inches [43 (45.5, 48.5, 49.5, 51, 53.5, 53.5, 53.5) cm]

D- Yoke: 8¼ (9½, 9¾, 9¾, 10½, 10¾, 11, 11¼) inches [21 (24, 24.75, 24.75, 26.75, 27.5, 28, 28.5) cm]

E- Total length: 23¼ (25½, 26¼, 26¾, 28½, 29¾, 31, 31¼) inches [59 (64.75, 66.5, 68, 72.5, 75.5, 78.75, 79.5) cm]

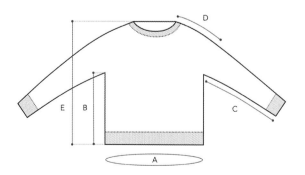

GRETA CHART 1

GRETA CHART 2

GRETA CHART 3

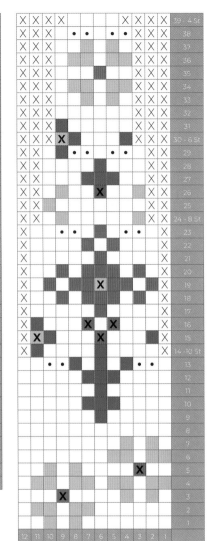

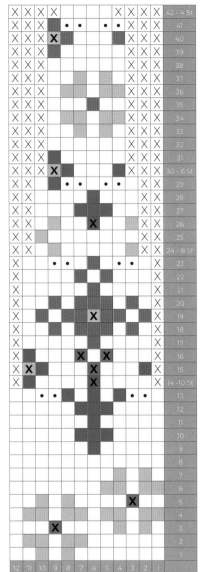

KEY

| x | = No stitch |

| • | = Decrease by knitting the two dots together |

| **X** | = Knit with MC and duplicate stitch later |

| □ | = Main Color (MC) |

| ▨ | = Contrasting Color 3 (CC3) |

| ▧ | = Contrasting Color 2 (CC2) |

| ▩ | = Contrasting Color 1 (CC1) |

LITTLE GRETA PULLOVER

❉ ❉ ❉ INTERMEDIATE 1

I love this cheerful little yoke sweater. It reminds me of the flowery wreaths and joyful primary colors of Midsommar. It's the kind of sweater you can knit in the dark of winter, when the vibrant colors of summer seem like a far-off dream. Plus, I love sweaters you can wear on chilly summer nights and not look like it's Christmas in July. Little Greta is knit in the round, bottom up. Like the Greta Pullover (page 107), the yoke may look a bit tricky with those three- and four-color rows, but you can simply knit with two colors and add the other colors afterward with a duplicate stitch. More experienced knitters can knit those rows holding three colors at once. Little Greta is knit with Biches & Bûches Le Gros Lambswool, which adds a bulky yet soft and light feel that your little one will love. It's snuggly like a blanket.

SKILLS YOU'LL PRACTICE

Long-tail cast on (page 184). Duplicate stitch join (page 183). Joining in the round seamlessly (page 37). Working 1x1 ribbing (k1, p1). DPN work for the sleeves. Backward loop increase (page 182). Splicing yarn (page 186). Joining body and sleeves onto one needle. Weaving a new yarn color in (and out) (pages 38–39 and 44–45). Knitting two colors in the round, left and right together (pages 41–42). Reading a chart (page 9). Catching floats (pages 85–87). K2tog decrease (page 184). Ssk decrease (page 186). Kitchener stitch (page 183). Duplicate stitch for extra colors (page 183).

SIZES

Child's S (M, L) to fit US 4–6 (7–10, 12–14) / [110 (120–130, 140) cm]

A generous fit of 3–9 inches (7.5–23 cm) positive ease (built-in growing room)

MATERIALS

YARN: Aran | Biches & Bûches Le Gros Lambswool | 100% Scottish Lambswool | 210 yards (192 m) per 3.5-ounce (100-g) skein

MAIN COLOR (MC): Undyed Off-White | 3 (3, 4) skeins [450 (525, 625) yards] / [411 (480, 571) m]

CONTRASTING COLOR 1 (CC1): Medium Blue | 1 skein [30 (32, 34) yards] / [27 (29, 31) m]

CONTRASTING COLOR 2 (CC2): Medium Red | 1 skein [28 (30, 32) yards] / [25 (27, 29) m]

CONTRASTING COLOR 3 (CC3): Dark Yellow | 1 skein [12 (13, 14) yards] / [11 (12, 13) m]

NEEDLES: One 32-inch (80-cm) or 40-inch (100-cm) circular needle for the body and one set of double-pointed needles (DPNs), FlexiFlips, or a 16-inch (40-cm) circular needle for the sleeves in size needed to obtain gauge in colorwork and single color

SUGGESTED NEEDLE SIZE: US 7 (4.5 mm)

One 32-inch (80-cm) or 40-inch (100-cm) circular needle for the body ribbing and one set of double-pointed needles (DPNs), FlexiFlips, or a 16-inch (40-cm) circular needle for the ribbing on the sleeves one size smaller than gauge-size needle

SUGGESTED NEEDLE SIZE: US 6 (4 mm)

ADDITIONAL MATERIALS

Stitch marker, measuring tape, scissors, and tapestry needle

GAUGE AND SWATCH

16 stitches and 19 rounds = 4 inches (10 cm)

Please swatch in the round to determine needle size.

> **NOTE:** Swatch in both one color and in colorwork. You may need to knit the single-color part of the sweater with a smaller needle than the colorwork section. The gauge is the same throughout the sweater.

FINISHED MEASUREMENTS

CHEST: 29½ (31½, 33½) inches [75 (80, 85) cm]

BODY LENGTH TO UNDERARM: 10½ (13, 14) inches [26.5 (33, 35.5) cm]

SLEEVE LENGTH: 9¾ (12½, 13½) inches [25 (32, 34.5) cm]

YOKE DEPTH: 5¼ (5¾, 6¼) inches [16.5 (14.5, 16) cm]

TOTAL LENGTH: 15¾ (18¾, 20½) inches [40 (47, 51.5) cm]

INSTRUCTIONS

1. CAST ON

With smaller needles and the MC, using a long-tail cast on, cast on 118 (126, 134) stitches.

2. RIBBING

Place a marker at the beginning of the round. Join for knitting in the round, being careful not to twist the cast-on stitches. Round 1: *Knit 1, purl 1.* Repeat from * to * all the way around. (Hint: Work the first 2 stitches with the working yarn and the tail from the long-tail cast on for a seamless join.) Work 1x1 ribbing for another 8 (8, 10) rounds.

3. KNIT BODY

Change to larger needles and knit in the round until the body measures 10½ (13, 14) inches [26.5 (33, 35.5) cm] or until the desired length to the underarm. Stop 4 (4, 4) stitches before the marker. Place the next 8 (8, 8) stitches onto a holder for the underarm.

4. KNIT SLEEVE

With smaller DPNs and the MC, cast on 32 (34, 36) stitches. Divide the stitches evenly between three DPNs. Place a marker and join by knitting from the last cast-on stitch to the first cast-on stitch. Work 1x1 ribbing (k1, p1) for 6 (7, 8) rounds. Next round, change to larger needles, knit 1, increase one stitch, and knit to the end of the round. Total stitches: 33 (35, 37). Continue to knit in the round for eight rounds. Increase one stitch right after the first stitch and before the last stitch of the round. Total stitches: 35 (37, 39). Increase 2 stitches in the same manner every 1 (1½, 1½) inch [2.5 (3.5, 3.5) cm] 3 (3, 3) times. Total stitches: 41 (43, 45). Continue knitting until the sleeve measures 9¾ (12½, 13½) inches [25 (32, 34.5) cm] or the desired length. On the last round, stop knitting 4 (4, 4) stitches before the marker. Place the next 8 (8, 8) stitches onto a holder for the underarm.

5. JOIN THE BODY TO THE FIRST SLEEVE FOR THE YOKE

Match up the stitches set aside for the underarm on the body to the stitches set aside for the underarm on the sleeve. Place a marker. Continuing with the yarn used for knitting the body, knit the left sleeve for 33 (35, 37) stitches. Knit across the front of the body for 51 (55, 59) stitches.

Place the next 8 (8, 8) stitches onto a holder for the second underarm. Now you are all ready to attach the second sleeve. Set work aside.

6. KNIT SECOND SLEEVE

Repeat Step 4 and knit the right sleeve.

7. JOIN SECOND SLEEVE TO THE BODY

Match up the stitches for the right underarm to the body. Knit from the front stitches to the 33 (35, 37) right-sleeve stitches. Continue knitting across 51 (55, 59) back stitches to the marker. Ta-da. You have joined the sleeves to the body and are ready to knit the yoke. Total stitches: 168 (180, 192). With the MC, knit - (2, 5) rounds.

8. KNIT THE YOKE AND DECREASE STITCHES

Now the fun starts. Carrying the CC in your left hand and the MC in your right hand (making sure that the contrasting color is in the dominant position), begin knitting the chart (page 117) on the right bottom corner. Repeat the chart 14 (15, 16) times per round. Work only two colors at once per round. Work the stitches for the third accent color marked with an X on the chart with the MC and add the appropriate color later with a duplicate stitch.

Work decreases as indicated by knitting the stitches marked with dots together. Work colorwork chart decreases as follows: Decrease rounds are Rounds 4, 13, 18, 22, and 23. There are two stitches decreased on each decrease round. Work the first decrease with a k2tog and work the second decrease with a ssk. Complete the chart. Total stitches: 56 (60, 64).

9. WORK NECKBAND

There are 56 (60, 64) stitches for the neckband. With the smaller needles and the MC, knit one round. Work 1x1 ribbing (k1, p1) for 7 (7, 7) rounds. Bind off all stitches in established 1x1 ribbing and decrease 4 stitches evenly spaced around the neck by working a purl and a knit stitch with a k2tog. Break yarn, leaving an 8-inch (20-cm) tail. Thread the tail of the yarn onto a tapestry needle. With a duplicate stitch, connect the last stitch of the round to the first stitch of the round.

10. FINISHING

With the appropriate color yarn and a tapestry needle, duplicate stitch the stitches marked with an X on the chart on top of the MC used to knit the stitch. (See duplicate stitch embroidery on page 55.) When adding a color, work all the way around the yoke on the same round as if you are knitting with that color, weaving in the strand of yarn with the tapestry needle to catch the floats, as needed. Weave in all the ends and graft together the underarm stitches using the Kitchener Stitch. Steam block. Congrats! Share this adorable sweater with one of your favorite little ones.

LITTLE GRETA SCHEMATIC

A- Chest circumference: 29½ (31½, 33½) inches [75 (80, 85) cm]

B- Body length to underarm: 10½ (13, 14) inches [26.5 (33, 35.5) cm]

C- Sleeve length: 9¾ (12½, 13½) inches [25 (32, 34.5) cm]

D- Yoke depth: 5¼ (5¾, 6¼) inches [16.5 (14.5, 16) cm]

E- Total length: 15¾ (18¾, 20½) inches [40 (47, 51.5) cm]

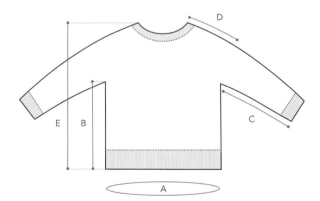

LITTLE GRETA CHART

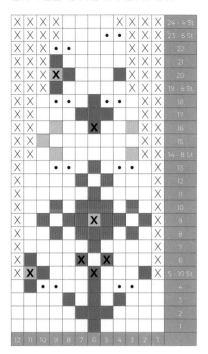

KEY

x = No stitch

• = Decrease by knitting the two dots together

X = Knit with MC and duplicate stitch later

☐ = Main Color (MC)

☐ = Contrasting Color 3 (CC3)

☐ = Contrasting Color 2 (CC2)

☐ = Contrasting Color 1 (CC1)

NORDIC MASTERCLASS

PURL WITH TWO COLORS, MAKE A FANCY BRAID, AND PREPARE FOR A LIFETIME OF COLORWORK

I believe in colorwork without limitations. It makes me sad when a talented colorwork knitter has to avoid a pattern they love, simply because they lack practice with a single skill. Often that skill is purling in colorwork. The main reason people avoid purling in colorwork is that you're working on the wrong side of the work, so you can't see and read your pattern as easily. In some ways, it's like knitting colorwork blind. The trick here is not to knit blind, but rather to learn to read the stitches on your left needle. That's the key. All of the projects in this section are designed to help you ease into purling with colorwork. You will gain purling skills and make some beautiful projects at the same time.

This chapter has some of the most varied and rewarding projects in the book, from classic Nordic sweaters with pewter clasps to Norwegian slippers and a traditional Selbu mitten. It also includes a fingerless mitt and even a whimsical throw pillow. Each project has just a few purling rows. So don't be scared away. Gently learn this skill with any one of these projects, and soon you'll be able to make any colorwork project on the planet and have the skills to conquer it.

Whichever you choose to knit, don't miss the tutorials. The colorwork purling tutorial is included in the Stjerne Slippers pattern (pages 123–124). There is also a tutorial there for the tvinnarand stitch. Tvinnarand is a cousin to the Latvian braid, but it has an extra twist. This decorative edge keeps knitwear from rolling. I love adding this Nordic touch to my designs, and you will too.

STJERNE SLIPPERS

✱✱✱✱ INTERMEDIATE 2

Stjerne means "star" in Norwegian. And star motifs are one of my favorite things about Nordic knitting. I love how Scandinavian symbolism allows us to handcraft gifts with meaning. Stars mean light and hope. Stars encourage us to let our light shine and to do our best. Stars promise light in darkness, guidance when we are lost, and protection from above. The purling in colorwork all happens at the beginning of this project as you knit the heel back and forth. It's a great place to learn because you are working over a small number of stitches, and you get to knit half the time. The check pattern is simple, and you'll catch on in a snap. I love to make star slippers for my loved ones to wear in winter. It's happy to think I'm keeping all my favorite feet cozy and reminding their owners of the light to come through the darkest time of year.

SKILLS YOU'LL PRACTICE

Mad gauge skills (page 9–10). Duplicate stitch join (page 183). Long-tail cast on (page 184). Knitting and purling with two colors, left and right together (pages 41–42 and 123–124). Reading a chart (page 9). K2tog decrease (page 184). Ssk decrease (page 186). Backward loop increase (page 182). Two-color long-tail cast on (pages 126–127). Joining in the round seamlessly (page 37). DPN work. Catching floats (pages 85–87). Sl1-k2tog-psso decrease (page 186). Running backstitch (page 186). Tvinnarand stitch (pages 130–131). Felting (page 132).

SIZES

Women's size M (to fit shoe size US 6–8 [Euro 36-39])

Men's size M (to fit shoe size US 8–11 [Euro 41-44])

MATERIALS

WOMEN'S SLIPPER

YARN: DK | Rauma Strikkegarn | 3-ply 100% Norwegian Wool | 114 yards (105 m) per 1.75-ounce (50-g) skein

MAIN COLOR (MC): 105 Charcoal | 1 skein [70 yards (64 m)]

CONTRASTING COLOR 1 (CC1): 101 Off-White | 1 skein [70 yards (64 m)]

CONTRASTING COLOR 2 (CC2): Red 128 | 1 skein [6 yards (5.5 m)]

MEN'S SLIPPER

YARN: Worsted | Harrisville Designs Highland Worsted | 100% Virgin Wool | 200 yards (182 m) per 3.5-ounce (100-g) skein

MAIN COLOR (MC): Charcoal | 1 skein [85 yards (78 m)]

CONTRASTING COLOR (CC1): Off-white | 1 skein [70 yards (64 m)]

CONTRASTING COLOR (CC2): Worsted | Harrisville Designs WATERshed | 100% Pure Virgin Wool | 110 yards (100 m) per 1.75-ounce (50-g) skein | Barndoor | 1 skein [8 yards (7 m)]

NEEDLES: Double-pointed needles (DPNs) or FlexiFlips in gauge-size needles

SUGGESTED NEEDLE SIZE: US 4 (3.5 mm) for women's slippers and US 4 (3.5 mm) for men's slippers. Needle size will vary widely. Please swatch.

GAUGE AND SWATCH

Swatch in colorwork.

WOMEN'S SLIPPER: 24 stitches and 24 rows = 4 inches (10 cm)

MEN'S SLIPPER: 19 stitches and 19 rows = 4 inches (10 cm)

If you need a larger size, determine gauge, then move up a needle size for a roomier slipper. I use a size US 3 (3.25 mm) for a women's size small (to fit US shoe size 5–7 / Euro 36–38) and a size US 5 (4 mm) for a women's size large (to fit US shoe size 8–10 / Euro size 39–41). I use a size 4 (3.5 mm) for a men's size medium (to fit US shoe size 8–11 / Euro 43–45). Keep that in mind. If you need a smaller size, go down a needle size (from gauge) or shrink them a bit with extra felting in hot water. Yardage will vary slightly when you alter the gauge, but there is plenty of yarn in each skein for all sizes.

FINISHED MEASUREMENTS

WOMEN'S M (TO FIT US SHOE SIZE 6–8 [EURO 36–39])

UNFELTED SLIPPER: 5¼ x 10 inches (13.5 x 25.5 cm)

FELTED SLIPPER: approximately 4½ x 9¼ inches (11.5 x 23.5 cm)

MEN'S M (TO FIT US SHOE SIZE 8–11 [EURO 41–44])

UNFELTED SLIPPER: 6½ x 12¾ inches (16.5 x 32.5 cm)

FELTED SLIPPER: 5½ x 10 inches (14 x 25.5 cm)

INSTRUCTIONS

1. CAST ON

With the CC1, using a long-tail cast on, cast on 32 stitches.

2. BEGIN HEEL—ROW 1

The heel is worked back and forth in stockinette with two DPNs. The first row is worked on the wrong side of the slipper. Knit one row. Turn work.

3. BEGIN COLORWORK AND KNIT HEEL— ROWS 2–41

Add the MC and work the second row of the chart (page 133). See the colorwork purling tutorial on the adjacent page.

> **NOTE:** For the heel (Rows 3–41), the odd number rows will be purled and the even number rows will be knit. Carry the CC1 in your left hand and the MC in your right hand. This is so the pattern yarn is in the dominant position. (If you are carrying the yarn in one hand, carry the CC1 to the left of the MC.) Beginning on Row 6 of the heel, decreases and increases occur on every knit row. Ssk for the first decrease and k2tog for the second decrease. Pay attention to the pattern and increase and decrease the stitches in the correct color of yarn to continue the pattern to the edge of the slipper. To make new stitches, use the backward loop cast on.

PURLING IN COLORWORK WITH THE RIGHT HAND

1.

Place the right needle as to purl.

2.

With your right hand, wrap the MC from around the back.

3.

Pull through.

4.

Complete the stitch.

PURLING IN COLORWORK WITH THE LEFT HAND

1.

Insert the right needle as to purl, and lay the white yarn (CC1) over the top of the right needle.

2.

With your left thumb, pull the CC1 down to anchor the CC1.

3.

Bring the CC1 back through the stitch.

4.

Complete the purl stitch.

4. CAST ON STITCHES FOR THE INSTEP—ROW 42

On Row 42: Following the chart, knit across the 32 stitches for the bottom of the foot. Onto a new DPN, cast on 31 stitches for the instep in the following manner: Pick up the working yarn and set up for a long-tail cast on (please see the tutorial on page 126) with the MC over your index finger and the CC over your thumb. Cast on 31 stitches, alternating the CC1 and MC stitches for the instep. To change colors, twist the yarn clockwise and place the CC1 on your index finger and the MC on your thumb. Whichever color is over your index finger will be the color of the stitch. Fold the slipper in two, so the needles run parallel to each other. Total stitches: 63. From Round 43 on, the slipper is knit in the round.

TWO-COLOR LONG-TAIL CAST ON

1.

Put the MC yarn over your index finger to set up for a long-tail cast on.

2.

Loop the CC over your thumb to set up for a long-tail cast on.

3.

Go under the thumb loop and over the MC yarn.

4.

Grab the MC yarn and bring it back through the thumb loop.

5.

Pull to tighten the stitch.

6.

Switch yarn so that the CC1 is over your index finger . . .

7.

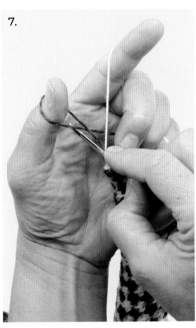

. . . and the MC is looped over your thumb.

8.

Go up through the thumb loop with the right needle.

9.

Grab the CC1 off your index finger and pull through the loop.

10.

Pull to tighten the stitch.

6. TOE SHAPING—ROUNDS 70–82

Continue knitting in the round, following the chart. On Round 70, the decrease is only on the sole of the foot. From Round 71 on, you will decrease 4 stitches on every row as indicated on the chart. Stitches 1 and 32 on the bottom of the foot and Stitches 36 and 60 on the top of the foot are hero stitches (stitches that travel to create an outline) and are knit with the CC1. Round 77: Consolidate all the stitches for the top and bottom of the foot onto two needles. Row 82: On the top of the front toe, slip one stitch, k2tog, and pass the slipped stitch over the knit stitch. Knit to the end of the row.

7. HOMESTRETCH

Break the yarn and thread a tapestry needle with both colors. With the tapestry needle, run both colors through the live stitches. Pull to gather. Insert the needle through the hole at the top of the toe. Turn the slipper inside out. Pull to gather again and weave in the ends separately to secure. Weave in all the ends. With right sides facing, sew the sides of the heel together with a running backstitch.

8. TVINNARAND ROUNDS (NORWEGIAN TWISTING ROUNDS)

With the CC1, begin at the left side of the slipper and pick up and knit 49 stitches across the instep and around the top of the heel to make a decorative cuff. Join to knit in the round and work two rounds of tvinnarand referring to the photos on pages 130–131. Tvinnarand is similar to a Latvian braid with a twisted purl stitch. Tvinnarand is worked with two colors.

Step 1: Start with both strands in front of the work (see Photo 1, page 130). The CC2 is on the top and the CC1 is on the bottom.

Step 2: Round 1 of tvinnarand: Switch the position of the yarn by rotating your wrist away from you, so your thumb is on the top and your index finger is on the bottom. Begin with the CC1 strand, and hold the CC2 down and out of the way with your right thumb (see Photo 2, page 130).

5. REDISTRIBUTE STITCHES ONTO FOUR NEEDLES AND KNIT IN THE ROUND—ROUNDS 43–69

Round 43: With Needle 1, join the last cast-on stitch for the instep to the first stitch of the sole. Knit across the first 16 stitches of the bottom of the foot. With Needle 2, knit across Stitches 17–32. With Needle 3, knit across the first half of the instep (Stitches 33–48). With Needle 4, knit Stitches 49–63. Continue knitting Rounds 64–69. Catch floats where necessary.

Step 3: Insert the needle as to purl and catch the strand under the needle with a downward motion (see Photo 3, page 130), and pull back through the loop (not a traditional purl—this way it twists the stitch).

Step 4: Complete the tvinnarand stitch. Now the two strands of yarn run horizontally in front of the work, with the CC1 on top and the CC2 beneath (see Photo 4, page 130).

Step 5: You need to switch the position of the strands by bringing the CC2 over the CC1 and rotating your wrist away from you in a counterclockwise twist (see Photo 5, page 131).

Step 6: Purl the next tvinnarand stitch with the CC2 strand (see Photo 6, page 131).

Step 7: Switch positions of the strands with a counterclockwise twist and purl a tvinnarand stitch with the CC1 just like the first stitch (see Photo 2, page 130). Continue in this manner all the way around, alternating colors and twisting the yarn counterclockwise between each twisted-purl stitch.

NOTE: The strands will become twisted along the way. Adjust them occasionally to make them easier to work with.

Round 2: Begin with the CC1 and work in the same manner as Round 1, alternating colors, but on Round 2, rotate your wrist toward your body to twist the yarn clockwise (see Photo 7, page 131). When done correctly, the tvinnarand stitch looks like this (see Photo 7, page 131).

WORKING A TVINNARAND EDGE

1.

Start with both strands in front of the work, CC2 on top and CC1 on the bottom.

2.

Switch the position of the yarns by rotating your wrist away from you so your thumb is on top and your index finger is on the bottom.

3.

Purl with the yarn under the needle so it twists the stitch.

4.

Complete the tvinnarand stitch with the CC1.

5.

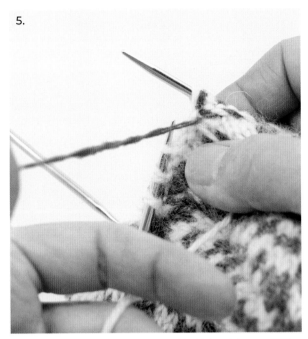

Rotate the yarns counterclockwise, and hold the white yarn (CC1) out of the way with your right thumb.

6.

Purl the CC2 yarn under the right needle, twisting the purl stitch.

7.

On the second round, twist the yarns clockwise. When done correctly, the two rows of tvinnarand make a row of horizontal Vs.

9. BIND OFF TVINNARAND ROUND AND FINISH

With the CC2, bind off the tvinnarand round. Break the yarn and thread the tail of the yarn onto a tapestry needle. Make one duplicate knit stitch to connect the last stitch of the bind off to the beginning stitch of the bind off in order to make the bind-off round appear seamless. Weave in ends on the wrong side.

10. MAKE A SECOND SLIPPER

Follow Steps 1–9 to make a second slipper. Woo-hoo! You're done!

11. FELT

Gently felt by washing the slippers using a short delicate cycle in your washing machine. Block. Dry flat. Do not dry in the dryer.

STJERNE SCHEMATIC

A- Circumference: 10½ (13) inches [26.5 (33) cm] unfelted, 9 (11) inches [22.5 (28) cm] felted

B- Length: 10 (12¾) inches [25.5 (32.5) cm] unfelted, 9¼ (10) inches [23.5 (25.5) cm] felted

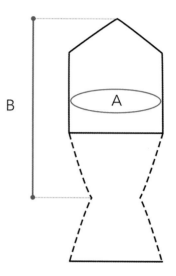

KEY

x	= No stitch
⟍	= ssk
⟋	= k2tog
•	= Knit (wrong side)
▲	= Backward loop/Long-tail cast on for instep
⋀	= sl1-k2tog-psso
	= CC1
▧	= MC

CHART

LITTLE HAAKON SWEATER

✹ ✹ ✹ ✹ INTERMEDIATE 2

This adorable child's sweater is 98 percent easy (two-star knitting) with just 2 percent purling in colorwork (four-star knitting). It's proof that a little color can go a long way—and that a little purling in colorwork can allow you to make some spectacular knits. This sweater reminds me of something Lise and Lasse would wear in the classic children's book *Children of the Northlights*. If the instructions appear lengthy, it's only because I walk you through the construction step-by-step. But it's not hard. The Little Haakon Sweater is knit with cozy Biches & Bûches Le Gros Lambswool. The wool for this rustic yarn is from Scotland, then spun in France. In Norway they say, "Det finnes ikke dårlig vær, bare dårlig klær," which means, "There is no bad weather, only bad clothes." This soft yet hardy yarn will keep your child warm in any weather. And the Little Haakon Sweater knits up in a flash!

SKILLS YOU'LL PRACTICE

Long-tail cast on (page 184). Splicing yarn (page 186). Joining in the round seamlessly (page 37). Knitting in the round. Working 1x1 ribbing (k1, p1). Stockinette stitch. Knitting and purling with two colors, left and right together (pages 41–42 and 123–124). Reading a chart (page 9). K2tog decrease (page 184). Ssk decrease (page 186). Three-needle bind off (page 187). Picking up stitches (page 186). Binding off (page 182). DPN work.

SIZES

Child's S (M, L, XL)

US 3–4 (4–6, 7–10, 12–14) or Euro sizes 110 (120, 130, 140) cm

MATERIALS

YARN: Aran | Biches & Bûches Le Gros Lambswool | 100% Scottish Lambswool | 210 yards (192 m) per 3.5-ounce (100-g) skein

MAIN COLOR (MC): Dark Grey | 2 (3, 3, 4) skeins [400 (499, 522, 648) yards] / [366 (457, 478, 593) m]

CONTRASTING COLOR (CC): Medium Red | 1 skein [45 (49, 53, 56) yards] / [41 (45, 49, 51) m]

NEEDLES: One 24-inch or 32-inch (60-cm or 80-cm) circular needle and one pair of double-pointed needles (DPNs), FlexiFlips, or a 16-inch (40-cm) circular needle for sleeves in size needed to obtain gauge in colorwork and single color

SUGGESTED NEEDLE SIZE: US 8 (5 mm)

One 24-inch or 32-inch (60-cm or 80-cm) circular needle one size smaller than gauge-size needle and one pair of DPNs or FlexiFlips to work ribbing

SUGGESTED NEEDLE SIZE: US 7 (4.5 mm)

ADDITIONAL MATERIALS

Stitch markers, measuring tape, scissors, tapestry needle, sewing needle, thread, and 1 or 2 pairs of clasps

GAUGE AND SWATCH

15 stitches and 20 rounds = 4 inches (10 cm)

Please swatch in the round to determine needle size.

FINISHED MEASUREMENTS

CHEST: 26¼ (28¼, 29¼, 30½) inches [66.75 (71.75, 24.25, 77.5) cm]

SLEEVE LENGTH: 11½ (12¼, 13¾, 16) inches [29 (31, 35, 40.5) cm]

BODY LENGTH: 15¾ (17, 18½, 20½) inches [40 (43, 47, 52) cm]

EASE: 3–5 inches (7.5–12.75 cm) positive ease

INSTRUCTIONS

1. CAST ON

With smaller needles and MC, using a long-tail cast on, cast on 98 (106, 110, 114) stitches.

2. RIBBING

Place marker at the beginning of the round. The beginning of the round is the left side of the sweater. Join the last cast-on stitch to the first cast-on stitch, being careful not to twist the cast-on stitches. Round 1: *Knit 1, purl 1.* Work from * to * all the way around. Continue to work 1x1 ribbing until ribbing measures 1¾ (2, 2, 2) inches [4.5 (5, 5, 5) cm].

3. KNIT BODY

Knit onto the larger needles and knit in the round until the body measures 10½ (11½, 12½, 14¼) inches [26.5 (29, 32, 37) cm].

4. SPLIT BACK AND FRONT AND KNIT BACK OF SWEATER

Knit across 49 (53, 55, 57) front stitches. Place front stitches onto a holder. Knit across 49 (53, 55, 57) back stitches. Turn and work flat in stockinette until the back of the sweater measures 14 (15¼, 16¾, 18¾) inches [35.5 (38.5, 42.5, 47.5) cm] or 1¾ inches (4.5 cm) short of the total desired length of the body, and after completing a purl row (WS).

Work colorwork from Chart 1 (page 141) for the back in stockinette for 10 rows. On the RS, begin with Stitch 1 (5, 1, 6) and end with Stitch 1 (3, 1, 2).

ROW 1: (RS) Knit in colorwork. Begin with Stitch 1 (5, 1, 6). Read the chart right to left. Turn.

ROW 2: (WS) Purl in colorwork. Begin with Stitch 1 (3, 1, 2). Read the chart left to right. Turn.

ROW 3: (RS) Knit in colorwork. Begin with Stitch 1 (5, 1, 6). Turn.

ROW 4: (WS) Purl in the CC. Slide work from the right needle along the cable to the left needle.

ROW 5: (WS again) Purl in MC. Now the MC is on the same side as the CC. Turn.

ROW 6: (RS) Knit in colorwork. Begin with Stitch 1 (5, 1, 6). Turn.

ROW 7: (WS) Purl with the CC only. Slide work from the right needle along the cable to the left needle.

ROW 8: (WS again) Purl with the MC. Turn.

ROW 9: (RS) Knit with the CC. Slide the work from the right needle along the cable to the left needle.

ROW 10: (RS again) Knit with the MC.

TOTAL LENGTH: 15¾ (17, 18½, 20¼) inches [40 (43, 47, 51.5) cm].

Place 16 (17, 17, 18) right back shoulder stitches onto a holder. Place 16 (17, 17, 18) left back shoulder stitches onto a holder. Place center 17 (19, 21, 21) stitches on a holder for the neckband. Set aside.

5. KNIT FRONT OF SWEATER

With the MC and larger needles, knit across the front of the sweater. Turn and purl one row. For sizes L and XL work flat in stockinette for - (-, 1, 1) inch [- (-, 2.5, 2.5) cm] after completing a purl row. Turn.

6. SEPARATE RIGHT AND LEFT FRONT OF SWEATER

With RS facing, knit across 24 (26, 27, 28) stitches and bind off one stitch for the center neck. Knit 23 (25, 26, 27) stitches. (Hint: The second stitch for the bind off is actually the first stitch on the right front of the sweater. So both the right and the left sides have 24 [26, 27, 28] stitches.) Place the left front stitches onto a holder.

7. WORK RIGHT FRONT STITCHES

Turn and work right front stitches. Work in stockinette until right front measures 14 (15¼, 16¾, 18¾) inches [35.5 (38.5, 42.5, 47.5) cm] from cast-on edge or 1¾ inches (4.5 cm) short of the total desired length for the body after completing a purl row.

8. WORK NECK SHAPING FOR THE RIGHT FRONT AND WORK COLORWORK FROM CHART 1

Continue working flat and shape the neckline. Colorwork is located along the shoulder. Occasionally two rows will be purled or knit consecutively in order to knit with one color at a time. Work with only the stitches for the right front on a circular needle so that you can knit/purl two rows consecutively as directed.

ROW 3: (RS) Bind off 2 stitches. Begin on Stitch 2 (1, 1, 6) and knit in colorwork. Turn. Total stitches: 18 (19, 19, 20).

ROW 4: (WS) Purl row with the CC. Slide work from the right needle along the cable to the left needle.

ROW 5: (WS again) Purl row with the MC. Turn.

ROW 6: (RS) Bind off one stitch. Beginning with Stitch 3 (2, 2, 1), knit in colorwork to the end of the row. Turn. Total stitches: 17 (18, 18, 19).

ROW 7: (WS) Purl row with the CC. Slide work from the right needle along the cable to the left needle.

ROW 8: (WS again) Purl row with the MC. Turn.

ROW 9: (RS) Bind off one stitch and knit with the CC. Slide work from the right needle along the cable to the left needle. Total stitches: 16 (17, 17, 18).

ROW 10: (RS again) Knit row with the MC.

Total neck decrease over 10 rows is 8 (9, 10, 10) stitches.

Place right front 16 (17, 17, 18) stitches onto a holder.

9. WORK LEFT FRONT OF SWEATER AFTER SPLIT

With RS facing, knit 24 (26, 27, 28) stitches. Turn and work left front in stockinette, until left front measures 14 (15¼, 16¾, 18¾) inches [35.5 (38.5, 42.5, 47.5) cm] from cast-on edge, or 1¾ inches (4.5 cm) short of the total desired length for the body after completing a knit row.

ROW 1: (WS) Purl and, with the MC, bind off the first 4 (5, 6, 6) stitches. Begin colorwork on Stitch 2 (3, 3, 4) of Chart 1. Work in colorwork to the end of the row. Turn. Total stitches: 20 (21, 21, 22). (Hint: Purl rows are read from left to right.)

ROW 1: (RS) With the MC, bind off the first 4 (5, 6, 6) stitches. Begin colorwork on Row 1 of Chart 1 with Stitch 6 (5, 5, 4). Work in colorwork to the end of the row, ending with Stitch 1. (Hint: Knit rows are read from right to left on the chart.) Turn. Total stitches: 20 (21, 21, 22).

ROW 2: (WS) Purl row and work Row 2 of colorwork. Begin on Stitch 1. Turn. (Hint: Purl rows are read left to right on the chart.)

ROW 2: (RS) Knit row, keeping pattern correct in colorwork. Start on Stitch 1. (Hint: Knit rows are read right to left on the chart.) Turn.

ROW 3: (WS) Bind off 2 stitches. Begin with Stitch 6 (1, 1, 2) and purl in colorwork to the end of the row. Turn. Total stitches: 18 (19, 19, 20).

ROW 4: (RS) Knit row with the CC. Slide work from the right needle along the cable to the left needle.

ROW 5: (RS again) Knit row with the MC. Turn.

ROW 6: (WS) Bind off one stitch. Begin with Stitch 5 (6, 6, 1) and purl in colorwork to the end of the row. Turn. Total stitches: 17 (18, 18, 19).

ROW 7: (RS) Knit row with the CC. Slide work from the right needle along the cable to the left needle.

ROW 8: (RS again) Knit row with the MC. Turn.

ROW 9: (WS) Bind off one stitch and purl with the CC. Slide work from the right needle along the cable to the left needle. Total: 16 (17, 17, 18) stitches.

ROW 10: (WS again) Purl row with the MC.

Total neck decrease over 10 rows is 8 (9, 10, 10) stitches.

Place left front 16 (17, 17, 18) stitches onto a holder.

10. JOIN SHOULDER SEAMS

Place 16 (17, 17, 18) stitches for right back onto a DPN and 16 (17, 17, 18) right front stitches onto a second DPN. With the right sides facing, join shoulders with a three-needle bind off.

Repeat for the left side.

11. PICK UP AND KNIT SLEEVE

With the MC, starting at the right underarm, pick up and knit 40 (42, 44, 48) stitches, working around the right armhole for the right sleeve. Place a marker at the underarm to mark the beginning of the round. Knit one round, beginning on Stitch 6 (5, 4, 2) of Chart 2 (page 141) and ending on Stitch 3 (4, 5, 1). Knit Rounds 1–9 in colorwork.

With the MC, knit for 1 inch (2.5 cm).

Work decrease round: Knit 1, k2tog, knit to 3 stitches before marker, ssk, k1 (2 stitches decreased).

Knit seven rounds.

WORK DECREASE ROUND: Knit 1, k2tog, knit to 3 stitches before marker, ssk, k1 (2 stitches decreased).

Continue sleeve, working a decrease round every 1 inch (2.5 cm) 5 (6, 5, 6) times until you have 28 (28, 32, 34) stitches. Continue to knit sleeve until the sleeve measures 9 (9¾, 11¼, 13½) inches [23 (25, 28.5, 34) cm].

Work Chart 3 (page 141) beginning on Stitch 1.

With smaller needles, knit 1x1 ribbing (k1, p1) for 2 inches (5 cm).

Bind off all stitches. Break the yarn, leaving a 6-inch (15.25-cm) tail. Thread the tail of the yarn onto a tapestry needle. Connect the last bound-off stitch to the first bound-off stitch with a duplicate stitch. Weave in the tail.

12. KNIT SECOND SLEEVE

Repeat Step 11 and knit the left sleeve.

13. WORK NECKBAND

With RS facing, using smaller circular needles and MC, pick up approximately 15 (16, 17, 17) stitches along the right front neckline and pick up and knit one stitch at the top of the shoulder. Knit 17 (19, 21, 21) stitches across the back stitches on the holder, then pick up and knit one stitch at the top of the shoulder and 15 (16, 17, 17) stitches down the left front. Total stitches: 49 (53, 57, 57). Work Chart 4 (page 141) in stockinette.

ROW 1: (WS) Purl in colorwork starting on Stitch 6 (5, 1, 1) of Chart 4. Read the chart from left to right. Turn. Total stitches: 49 (53, 57, 57). End on Stitch 6 (1, 5, 5).

ROW 2: (RS) With the CC, knit in colorwork beginning on Stitch 6 (1, 5, 5). Read the chart from right to left. End on Stitch 6 (5, 1, 1). Turn.

ROW 3: (WS) Purl Row 3 in colorwork beginning on Stitch 6 (5, 1, 1). Turn.

ROW 4: (RS) Knit in colorwork beginning on Stitch 6 (1, 5, 5). Turn.

ROW 5: (WS) Purl in colorwork beginning on Stitch 6 (5, 1, 1). Turn.

ROW 6: (RS) Knit with the MC, cut the CC, and weave in the tail. Turn.

ROW 7: (WS) With the MC, purl to the end of the row. Turn.

ROW 8: (RS) Purl with the MC as turning row. Turn.

ROW 9: (WS) Purl with the MC and continue to work five rows in stockinette.

Bind off all stitches. Keep tension even and consistent with gauge. Break the yarn and leave a long tail to use for sewing.

Fold the neckband at the turning row and, using the tail, sew the neckband down to the inside of the sweater with a whipstitch.

14. WORK FRONT BANDS

Starting at the bottom of the right front opening, using the smaller needle, pick up and knit stitches along the front band edge. Pick up 3 stitches for every four knit rows from the bottom of the front band to the top of the neckband. Turn.

ROW 1: (WS) Purl one row. Turn.

ROW 2: (RS) Purl one row for a folding row. Turn.

ROWS 3–6: (WS) Starting with a purl row, work four rows in stockinette.

ROW 7: Bind off all stitches.

Fold the neckband at the turning row to the inside of the sweater and fasten the inside edge on the wrong side. Fasten the short side of the front band to the cast-off center stitch.

Pick up and work the left side in the same manner. On the left side, start at the top of the neckband edge.

15. SEW ON CLASPS

If using one pair of clasps, sew on clasps at the base of the neckband with the hook on the right side and the eye on the left side. If using two pairs of clasps, sew one clasp pair at the base of the neckband and the other pair of clasps at the center of the front bands.

16. FINISHING

Weave in all the remaining ends. Steam block. Give to a little Viking you love.

LITTLE HAAKON SCHEMATIC

A- Chest circumference: 26¼ (28¼, 29¼, 30½) inches [66.75 (71.75, 24.25, 77.5) cm]

B- Body length to underarm: 15¾ (17, 18½, 20½) inches [40 (43, 47, 52) cm]

C- Arms/sleeve depth: 5¼ (5½, 6, 6) inches [13.5 (14, 15, 15) cm]

D- Front slit length: 5½ (6, 6, 6) inches [14 (15, 15, 15) cm]

E- Sleeve length: 11½ (12¼, 13¾, 16) inches [29 (31, 35, 40.5) cm]

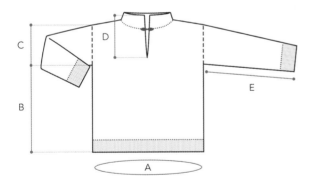

HAAKON CHART 1

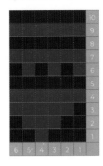

HAAKON CHART 2

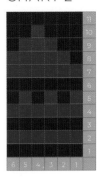

HAAKON CHART 3

HAAKON CHART 4

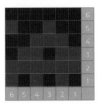

KEY

■ = Contrasting Color (CC)

■ = Main Color (MC)

OLSEN SLIPPERS

✳ ✳ ✳ ✳ INTERMEDIATE 2

In 1902, the Olsen family, including my great-grandpa Arthur Olsen, left Norway. The oldest child, a daughter, was married and stayed in Norway with her husband. Three of the older children were already in America, staying with family in Minnesota. At 12 years old, my grandpa Olsen was the oldest of the children to make the voyage in 1902. I designed this slipper, thinking of those little Olsen children, 12, 9, and 6, crossing the ocean to their new home. I included a traditional Selbu (eight-pointed) Star to represent Norway and a compass to represent the voyage. The sole of each slipper is a sea of stars to represent hope and light and to reflect the sky full of stars shining as they crossed the Atlantic. I used a super cozy American yarn, Harrisville Designs WATERshed, to represent my family bringing their Nordic traditions to their new life in America.

SKILLS YOU'LL PRACTICE

Long-tail cast on (page 184). Knitting and purling with two colors, left and right together (pages 41–42 and 123–124). Reading a chart (page 9). K2tog decrease (page 184). Ssk decrease (page 186). Backward loop increase (page 182). Two-color long-tail cast on (page 126). Joining in the round seamlessly (page 37). DPN work. Catching floats (pages 85–87). Sl1-k2tog-psso decrease (page 186). Running backstitch (page 186). Making a crochet edge (page 185). Felting.

SIZES

Children's sizes XS (S, M, L, XL) to fit US shoe sizes 5–7 (6.5–9.5, 10–13, 13–14) / Euro sizes 19–20 (23–24, 24–27, 28–32, 33–36)

MATERIALS

YARN: Worsted | Harrisville Designs WATERshed | 100% Pure Virgin Wool | 110 yards (100 m) per 1.75-ounce (50-g) skein

MAIN COLOR (MC): Barn Door | 1 skein [45 (50, 60, 64, 70) yards] / 41 (46, 55, 59, 64) m]

CONTRASTING COLOR (CC): Birch Bark | 1 skein [20 (22, 24, 26, 31) yards] / [18 (20, 22, 24, 28) m]

NEEDLES: Double-pointed needles (DPNs) or FlexiFlips in size needed to obtain gauge

SUGGESTED NEEDLE SIZE: US 4 (3.5 mm)

ADDITIONAL MATERIALS

Size G (4 mm) crochet hook, tapestry needle, scissors, and measuring tape

GAUGE AND SWATCH

24 stitches and 24 rows = 4 inches (10 cm)

Lightly felted to approximately 28 stitches and 24 rows = 4 inches (10 cm)

2. BEGIN HEEL

The heel is worked flat with two DPNs. The first row begins on the wrong side of the slipper. With the CC, knit one row. (On the chart on page 147 [147, 148, 149, 150], Row 1 is knit on the WS, so technically, the first row is worked in garter stitch.)

3. BEGIN COLORWORK AND KNIT HEEL— ROWS 2–17 (2–23, 2–27, 2–31, 2–35)

Turn work to work RS of slipper. Add the MC and knit Row 2 in colorwork. Purl Row 3 in colorwork. (See the tutorial on pages 123–124.)

For the heel portion, the odd number rows will be purled and the even number rows will be knit.

> **NOTE:** Carry the CC in your left hand and the MC in your right hand. This is so the pattern color is in the dominant position. If you are carrying the yarn in one hand, carry the CC to the left of the MC. Whichever method you use to knit with two colors, be consistent throughout the entire slipper.

INSTRUCTIONS

1. CAST ON

With the CC, using a long-tail cast on, cast on 19 (21, 23, 23, 23) stitches. Leave a long 9-inch (23-cm) tail to sew the heel together later.

ROW 6 (4, 4, 4, 4): Begin decreases for the heel. The first decrease is ssk and the second decrease is k2tog. Pay attention to the pattern and increase and decrease the stitches in the correct color of yarn to continue the pattern to the edge of the slipper. All increases and decreases are made on the knit side. To make new stitches, use the backward loop cast on.

4. CAST ON INSTEP—ROW 18 (24, 28, 32, 36)

ROW 18 (24, 28, 32, 36): Knit across the last row of the heel stitches. With the CC and the MC, using the two-color long-tail cast on (page 126), cast on 19 (21, 23, 23, 23) stitches onto a second DPN. Be careful to follow the chart. Fold the slipper in two, so the needles run parallel to each other. Total stitches: 38 (42, 46, 46, 46). From Round 19 (25, 29, 33, 37) on, the slipper is knit in the round.

5. REDISTRIBUTE STITCHES ONTO THREE NEEDLES AND KNIT ROUNDS 19–31 (25–39, 29–48, 33–53, 37–57)

ROUND 19 (25, 29, 33, 37): With Needle 1, join the last cast-on stitch for the instep to the first stitch of the sole and knit across the first half of the stitches for the bottom of the foot. With Needle 2, knit across the second half of the stitches for the bottom of the foot. With Needle 3, knit across the instep. Continue knitting in the round through Round 31 (39, 48, 53, 57).

6. TOE SHAPING—ROUNDS 32–38 (40–47, 49–57, 54–61, 58–66)

Continue knitting in the round, following the chart and decreasing 4 stitches on every round as indicated. The first decrease is ssk. The second decrease is k2tog. The third decrease is ssk, and the fourth decrease is k2tog. Notice on size M (XL) that the decrease begins on Round 49 (58) on the sole and on Round 50 (59) on the top of the foot.

ROUND 34 (43, 54, 56, 61): Consolidate all the stitches for the top and bottom of the foot onto two needles.

ROUND 38 (47, 57, 61, 66): Continue decreases on the sole, and for the final decrease on the top of the foot, slip one stitch, knit two together, and pass the slipped stitch over the knit stitch. Knit to the end of the row.

7. HOMESTRETCH

Break the yarn and thread a tapestry needle with both colors. With the tapestry needle, run both colors through the live stitches. Pull to gather. Insert the needle through the hole at the top of the toe. Turn the slipper inside out. Pull to gather again and weave in the ends separately to secure. Weave in all the ends.

Using the 9-inch (23-cm) cast-on tail, and right sides facing, sew the sides of the heel together. Sew down the right side of the heel with a running backstitch. Weave in the sewing yarn across the smallest part of the heel to get to the left side. Continue sewing the heel together on the left side with a running backstitch. Make sure your stitches are small so that there are no holes.

8. MAKE SECOND SLIPPER

Follow steps 1–7 to make the second slipper.

9. FINISHING

Gently felt by washing the slippers on a short delicate cycle in your washing machine. Block. Dry flat. Wrap up with a ribbon and give to a little person you love.

OLSEN SLIPPERS SCHEMATIC

A- Circumference: 6⅓ (7, 7⅔, 7⅔, 7⅔) inches [16 (17.75, 19.5, 19.5, 19.5) cm] before felting. Approximately 5½ (6, 6.5, 6.5, 6.5) inches [14 (15.25, 16.5, 16.5, 16.5) cm] after felting

B- Length: 4⅔ (5¾, 7, 7⅓, 8) inches [11.75 (14.5, 17.75, 18.5, 20.5) cm] before felting. Approximately 4½ (5¾, 6⅞, 7¼, 7¾) inches [11.4 (14.6, 17.5, 18.4, 19.6) cm] after felting

Turn the slipper right-side out and, with the CC, finish by crocheting across the instep. Begin on the left side, leaving a 6-inch (15.25-cm) tail to use to sew with later. Pick up and crochet one row of single crochet [approximately 10 (11, 12, 12, 13) stitches] across the instep. Break the yarn, leaving a 6-inch (15.25-cm) tail. Thread the tail of the yarn onto a tapestry needle. Make a duplicate stitch to connect the end of the crochet round to the first stitch on the heel (RS of slipper) in order to connect the crochet row to the cast-on row of the heel. There will appear to be a seamless crochet rim around the slipper. Connect the left side of the instep to the heel in the same manner.

Weave in the ends on the WS.

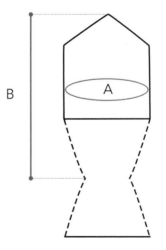

OLSEN XS CHART

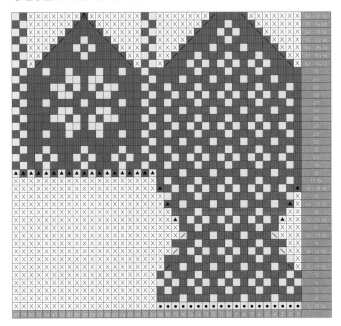

KEY

$\boxed{\text{x}}$ = No stitch

$\boxed{\diagdown}$ = ssk

$\boxed{\diagup}$ = k2tog

$\boxed{\bullet}$ = Knit on the WS

$\boxed{\blacktriangle}$ = Backward loop/Two-color long-tail cast on for instep

$\boxed{\wedge}$ = sl1-k2tog-psso

$\square$ = Contrasting Color (CC)

$\blacksquare$ = Main Color (MC)

OLSEN S CHART

SELBU MITTENS

✹ ✹ ✹ ✹ INTERMEDIATE 2

In 1857, a girl named Marit Gulsethbrua Emstad made three pairs of mittens featuring a centuries-old, eight-pointed star in bold black and white. She showed them off at church, and it wasn't long before a cottage industry sprung up, with her whole town making Selburose mittens for cold hands around the world. I designed these Selbu Mittens with my immigrant family in mind. When Norwegians immigrated to the United States, they packed a lot of knitwear because it was hard to find in the New World. I like to think of my grandmother's steamer trunk filled with treasures like these mittens. My mittens begin with a few rows of tvinnarand stitches. The two Selburoses represent my grandparents' homeland. There's a compass for the voyage to America and a starry palm that represents the sky full of stars they saw while crossing the Atlantic. The cuff and thumb feature a series of flowers to remind us all to bloom where we are planted.

SKILLS YOU'LL PRACTICE

Long-tail cast on (page 184). Two-color long-tail cast on (pages 126–127). Tvinnarand stitch (pages 130–131). Knitting with two colors, left and right together (pages 41–42). Reading a chart (page 9). K2tog decrease (page 184). Ssk decrease (page 186). Backward loop increase (page 182). Joining in the round seamlessly (page 37). DPN work. Catching floats (pages 85–87). Sl1-k2tog-psso decrease (page 186). Picking up stitches (page 186).

SIZES

Women's S/M, M/L

MATERIALS

YARN: Fingering | Rauma Finullgarn | 100% Norwegian Wool 2-ply | 191 yards (175 m) per 1.75-ounce (50-g) skein

MAIN COLOR (MC): 401 Natural White | 1 skein [90 (105) yards] / [82 (96) m]

CONTRASTING COLOR (CC): Color 410 Black | 1 skein [90 (105) yards] / [82 (96) m]

NEEDLES:
FlexiFlips, double-pointed needles (DPNs), or needles needed to obtain the correct gauge

SUGGESTED NEEDLE SIZE: US 2 (2.75 mm) for S/M and US 3 (3.25 mm) for M/L

ADDITIONAL MATERIALS

Scissors and tapestry needle

GAUGE AND SWATCH

GAUGE FOR WOMEN'S S/M: 29 stitches and 29 rows = 4 inches (10 cm)

GAUGE FOR WOMEN'S M/L: 27 stitches and 27 rows = 4 inches (10 cm)

FINISHED MEASUREMENTS

WOMEN'S S/M: 4 inches (10 cm) wide and 9¼ inches (23.5 cm) long

WOMEN'S M/L: 4¼ inches (10.75 cm) wide and 10 inches (25.5 cm) long

INSTRUCTIONS

1. CAST ON RIGHT-HAND MITTEN

With the MC, using a long-tail cast-on, cast on 50 stitches. Join for knitting in the round by knitting from the last stitch of the cast-on row to the first stitch of the cast-on row. Be careful not to twist the cast-on stitches. Knit one round.

2. TVINNARAND ROUNDS (NORWEGIAN BRAID)—ROUNDS 1–3

Tvinnarand is like a Latvian braid with a twisted purl stitch. (See the photo tutorial in the Stjerne Slippers pattern, page 130.) For the next two rounds, tvinnarand (twisted edge) is worked with two colors. Begin with Stitch 1 of Round 1 on the Right Mitten Chart (page 156): Start with both strands in front of the work. Begin with the MC strand and insert the needle as to purl, then catch the strand under the needle with a downward motion and pull back through the loop (not a traditional purl—this way it twists the stitch). Now, the two strands of yarn are running horizontally in front of the work, with the MC on top and the CC beneath. You need to switch the position of the strands by bringing the CC over the MC with a counterclockwise twist. Purl the next tvinnarand stitch with the CC strand, then switch the position of the strands with a counterclockwise twist, and purl a tvinnarand stitch with the MC strand. Continue in this manner all the way around, alternating colors and twisting the yarn counterclockwise between each twisted-purl stitch.

> **NOTE:** The strands will become twisted along the way. Adjust them occasionally to make it easier to work with.

Round 2 tvinnarand: Work in the same manner as Round 1, but twist the yarn clockwise. Round 3: With the MC, knit one round.

3. WORK COLORWORK—ROUNDS 4–13

Carry the CC in your left hand and the MC in your right hand. This is so that color used for the pattern is in the dominant position. If you are carrying the yarn in one hand, carry the CC to the left of the MC. Whichever method you use to knit with two colors, be consistent throughout the entire mitten. Follow the colorwork chart carefully. Catch the floats of the color being carried whenever there are 5 or more consecutive stitches of the same color in a row. Whenever there is almost an entire row of the background color, I like to catch the floats on every third stitch.

4. GUSSET AND THUMBHOLE—ROUNDS 14–33

On Round 14: Begin the gusset. Increase one stitch on each side of the thumb gusset with a backward loop as indicated on the chart. Continue following the chart to knit the mitten and to make the gusset increases. On Round 32, place 13 stitches onto a holder for the thumb and cast on 10 palm stitches with a two-color long-tail cast on as follows:

(continued)

Pick up the working yarn and set up for a long-tail cast on with the MC over your index finger and the CC over your thumb. See the tutorial on page 126. Cast on 1 MC, 1 CC, 3 MC, 1 CC, 3 MC, 1 CC. Total: 10 new palm stitches. To change colors, twist the yarn clockwise and place the CC on your index finger and the MC on your thumb. Whichever color is over your index finger will be the color of the stitch. Round 33: At the top of the gusset, knit 2 stitches together as marked on the chart.

5. CONTINUE KNITTING THE MITTEN—ROUNDS 34–55

Knit Rounds 34–55, catching floats where necessary.

6. SHAPING—ROWS 56–67

Continue knitting in the round, following the chart and decreasing 4 stitches on every round as indicated on the chart. The first and last MC stitches on the palm and back of the hand are hero stitches (stitches that travel to create an outline). All hero stitches are knit with the MC and will outline the mitten. Round 61: Consolidate the stitches onto two needles. Round 67: On the top of the mitten, knit 3 stitches, then slip 2 stitches individually, knit 1, and pass the slipped stitches over the knit stitch as indicated on the chart. Knit to the end of the round.

7. HOMESTRETCH

Break the yarn and thread a tapestry needle with both colors. With the tapestry needle, run both colors through the live stitches. Pull to gather. Insert the needle through the hole at the top of the mitten. Turn the mitten inside out. Pull to gather again and weave in the ends separately to secure. Weave in all the ends.

8. PICK UP THUMB STITCHES

Transfer the 13 thumb stitches on the holder to a DPN. Knit Round 1 across the 13 stitches for the back of the thumb (above the gusset), as indicated on the Thumb Chart (page 155). Keeping thumb pattern correct, with a second DPN, pick up and knit 2 stitches on the side, then pick up and knit 11 stitches across the top of the thumbhole and 2 stitches on the other side of the thumbhole. Continue knitting in the round, following the chart, with the flower pattern continuing above the gusset and the palm pattern on the back of the thumb. Be careful to match the pattern so that the pattern continues from the palm to the inside of the thumb. When the chart is completed, break the yarn and thread a tapestry needle with both colors. Run the tapestry needle through the live stitches. Pull to gather. Insert the needle through the hole at the top of the thumb and pull to gather again. Weave in the ends separately.

9. KNIT LEFT MITTEN

After knitting the right mitten, you know all the tricks. Follow the Left Mitten Chart (page 157) to knit the second mitten.

> **HINT:** On Round 32, place 13 stitches onto a holder for the thumb and cast on 10 palm stitches in this order: 1 CC, 3 MC, 1 CC, 3 MC, 1 CC, 1 MC.

10. FINISHING

Steam block. Gift or wear right away. I always encourage gifting slippers and mittens with a ribbon tied around them, but these black-and-white mittens look particularly stunning tied up with a colorful Norwegian ribbon.

SELBU MITTEN SCHEMATIC

WOMEN'S S/M

A- Circumference: 8 inches (20.5 cm)

B- Length: 9¼ inches (23.5 cm)

WOMEN'S M/L

A- Circumference: 8½ inches (21.5 cm)

B- Length: 10 inches (25.5 cm)

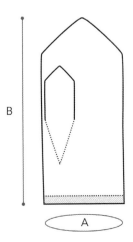

SELBU THUMB CHART

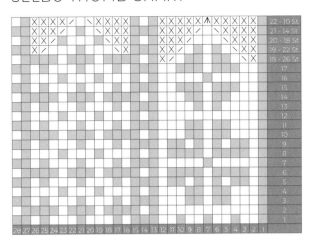

KEY

| x | = No stitch |

⟍ = ssk

⟋ = k2tog

— = Tvinnarand (Norwegian Braid)

• = Knit the two dots together

▲ = Backward loop/increase on gusset

⋀ = sl, sl, k1, psso

☐ = Main Color (MC)

■ = Stitches on holder

▨ = Contrasting Color (CC)

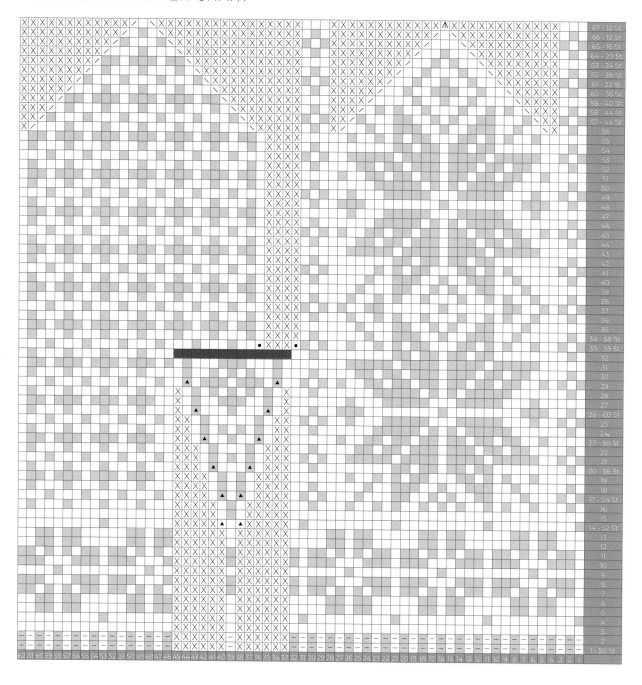

MIDSOMMAR PILLOW

✳ ✳ ✳ ✳ INTERMEDIATE 2

Midsommar Pillow is a festive knit that celebrates Sweden's summer solstice, when the sun never sleeps. Making this pillow is almost like painting by numbers. While it does require careful attention to the chart, it's incredibly fun to watch as a Viking ship, a Midsommar pole, and a Dala Horse emerge from your needles like magic. It's a very gratifying knit and not as hard as it may seem. The most challenging part is the first round of the chart. Count carefully to place the Swedish motifs correctly. After that, you can just knit from the Swedish row houses to the woven heart, to the man, to the woman, and so on. The back of the pillow is a simple checkerboard pattern that requires a little less concentration. I hope you'll give this whimsical pillow a try. It's a blast to knit.

SKILLS YOU'LL PRACTICE

Long-tail cast on (page 184). Joining in the round seamlessly (page 37). Weaving in new yarn (pages 38–39). Knitting and purling in two colors in the round, left and right together (pages 41–42 and 123–124). Mad chart-reading skills (page 9). Ssk decrease (page 186). Tvinnarand stitch (pages 130–131). Buttonholes (page 182). Backward loop increase (page 182). Catching floats (pages 85–87). Three-needle bind off (page 187). Binding off (page 182).

PRO TIP: Never catch a float on a stitch that has a float catch on the stitch directly below it. Alter the catch by at least one stitch or your catch will show through on the front.

MATERIALS

YARN: Aran | Biches & Bûches Le Gros Lambswool | 100% Scottish Lambswool | 210 yards (192 m) per 3.5-ounce (100-g) skein

MAIN COLOR (MC): Medium Blue | 2 skeins [252 yards (230 m)]

CONTRASTING COLOR (CC): Undyed White | 1 skein [126 yards (115 m)]

NEEDLES: One 32-inch (80-cm) circular needle in size needed to obtain gauge in colorwork

SUGGESTED NEEDLE SIZE: US 7 (4.5 mm)

One 32-inch (80-cm) circular needle one size smaller than gauge-size needle to use for single color knitting

SUGGESTED NEEDLE SIZE: US 6 (4 mm)

ADDITIONAL MATERIALS

Stitch markers, scissors, tapestry needle, 6 [¾-inch (2-mm)] buttons, 1 [20 x 20–inch (50 x 50–cm)] pillow, and 24 inches (60 cm) of decorative ribbon

GAUGE AND SWATCH

20 stitches and 20 rounds = 4 inches (10 cm) on larger needles

Please swatch in the round to determine needle size.

> **NOTE:** Swatch in both one color and in colorwork. You may need to knit the single-color part of the pillow with a smaller needle than the colorwork section.

FINISHED MEASUREMENTS

20 x 20 inches (51 x 51 cm)

INSTRUCTIONS

1. CAST ON

With larger needles, and MC, using a long-tail cast on, cast on 200 stitches.

2. JOIN FOR KNITTING IN THE ROUND

Round 1: Join for knitting in the round by knitting from the last cast-on stitch to the first cast-on stitch, being careful not to twist the cast-on stitches. Place marker A to mark the beginning of the round. Knit the first 2 stitches with working yarn and the cast-on tail for a seamless join. Knit to the end of the round. Rounds 2–4: Knit in the round with the MC. At the end of Round 4, stop knitting 7 stitches before the marker and weave in the CC in preparation for the colorwork.

3. WORK CHART 1 BOTTOM RIGHT AND BOTTOM LEFT (PAGES 167 AND 166) FOR THE FRONT AND CHART 2 (PAGE 163) FOR THE BACK OF THE PILLOW

The beginning of the round is located at the right side of the pillow. Knit Round 5 of Chart 1 Bottom Right (Stitches 1–50) on page 167. Place marker B. Continue to knit across Round 5 on Chart 1 Bottom Left (Stitches 51–100) on page 166. The first round of the pillow is very important, as it establishes the pattern for the entire pillow. Count the stitches carefully to place each motif in the correct position. Place marker C and work Round 1 of Chart 2 on page 163. Repeat the chart 12½ times across the back of the pillow to establish the checkerboard pattern.

Knit in the round, knitting from motif to happy motif on Chart 1, catching floats whenever there are more than five consecutive stitches of the same color in a row. You will have to catch the MC and the CC floats. This is the fun part, as the pictures appear on the front of the pillow. It's a bit like painting by numbers. Complete Chart 1 Bottom Right and Chart 1 Bottom Left and continue on Round 51 to work Chart 1 Top Right and Chart 1 Top Left (pages 165 and 164).

Complete Round 67 of Chart 1 Top Right and Chart 1 Top Left (at the top of the tulip). Stop knitting at marker C.

4. BIND OFF THE BACK OF THE PILLOW

Remove marker C. Knit, alternating the CC and the MC, and bind off 99 stitches across the back of the pillow to create the pillow closure on the back side of the pillow. Place the last stitch onto a holder to use later.

5. CAST ON AND KNIT BUTTONHOLE FLAP

With a new skein of MC yarn and gauge-size needles, WS facing, cast on 100 stitches for the hem of the buttonhole flap. Turn. With the CC and the MC, RS facing, work one row of tvinnarand stitches. Tvinnarand is like a Latvian braid with a twisted purl stitch. (See the photo tutorial in the Stjerne Slippers pattern, page 130.)

Tvinnarand stitches are worked with two colors. Start with both strands in front of the work. Begin with the CC strand and insert the needle as to purl, then catch the strand under the needle with a downward motion and pull back through the loop (not a traditional purl—this way it twists the stitch).

Now the two strands of yarn run horizontally in front of the work, with the CC on top and the MC beneath. You need to switch the position of the strands by bringing the MC over the CC with a counterclockwise twist. Purl the next tvinnarand stitch with the MC strand, then switch the position of the strands with a counterclockwise twist and purl a tvinnarand stitch with the CC. Continue in this manner all the way across the row, alternating colors and twisting the yarn counterclockwise between each twisted-purl stitch.

NOTE: The strands will become twisted along the way. Adjust them occasionally to make them easier to work with.

With WS facing and the MC, work two rows in stockinette. Make sure that you are on gauge (use smaller than gauge-size needle here). This is very important. If you are not on gauge, the hem of the flap will be floppy.

With WS facing, make six (three-stitch) buttonholes, evenly spaced, across the back of the pillow as follows: Purl 8 stitches, bind off 3 stitches, *purl 13, bind off 3.* Repeat from * to * four times. Purl 9 stitches. Keep in mind that the last bound-off stitch for each buttonhole is actually pulled over the first of the 13 purl stitches between each buttonhole. Turn and knit one row, adding 3 stitches with backward loops on top of each buttonhole. Work until one stitch remains in the row. Continue working with the yarn used to make the flap. With a ssk, join the last stitch of the buttonhole flap row to the stitch from the holder, making the last stitch on the buttonhole flap.

6. JOIN BUTTONHOLE FLAP TO THE FRONT OF THE PILLOW AND FINISH CHARTS 1 AND 2

Join the buttonhole flap to the front of the pillow. Knit with the CC and the MC. Work across Row 68 of Chart 1 Top Right and Chart 1 Top Left. Place marker C. Join the front of the pillow to the back of the pillow by knitting in the round and work Chart 2 beginning on Stitch 1. Continue to knit in the round with the CC and the MC until the last row of colorwork on Charts 1 (Top Right and Top Left) ending with the last stitch on Chart 2 on the back side of the pillow. Cut the CC and weave in the CC tail for 7 stitches and, with a smaller than gauge-size needle, knit four rounds with the MC.

Turn work. With WS facing, purl in colorwork and work Rows 1–4 of Chart 3 (page 163) in stockinette (purl on the WS and knit on the RS) to create a checkerboard pattern across the bottom of the buttonhole flap. Break the CC and weave in the tail to the back side of the flap.

7. FINISHING

Turn the pillow inside out and, with right sides facing, join the front of the pillow to the back of the pillow with the MC and a three-needle bind off.

With a tapestry needle and the MC, right sides facing, sew the bottom of the front of the pillow to the bottom of the back of the pillow with a running backstitch. Use small stitches so there are no gaps in the seam.

Weave in all the ends.

Turn the pillow right-side out and sew on the six buttons.

Make a facing for the inside of the buttonhole flap. With smaller needles and the CC, pick up and knit 93 stitches along the inside edge of the tvinnarand row. Work back and forth in stockinette for six rows. Bind off all stitches. Leave a long tail to use to sew the facing to the inside of the buttonhole flap. Thread the tail through a tapestry needle and neatly sew the facing to the buttonhole flap. Weave in the end.

Sew a decorative ribbon to the inside of the buttonhole flap, just under the buttonholes, covering up the edge of the facing. I love details like this!

Steam block your pillow to give the edges of the pillowcase a crisp line and to block the colorwork. Place a pillow inside the pillowcase and get ready to celebrate flowers, strawberries, long days, and short nights. This just might be the perfect thing for a midsummer nap!

MIDSOMMAR PILLOW SCHEMATIC

A- Circumference: 40 inches (101.5 cm)

B- 13½ inches (34.5 cm)

C- 6½ inches (16.5 cm)

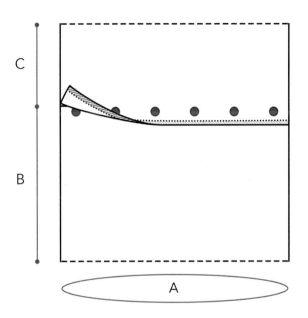

MIDSOMMAR CHART 2

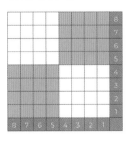

MIDSOMMAR CHART 3

KEY

☐ = Contrasting Color (CC)

▨ = Main Color (MC)

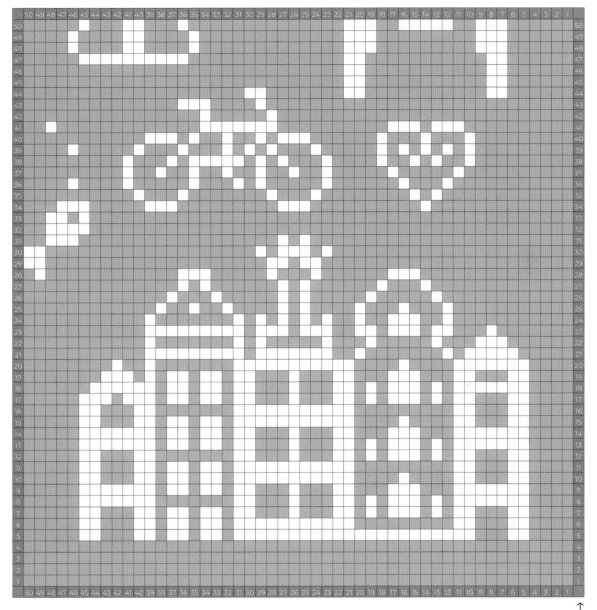

↑
BEGIN HERE

INGRID FINGERLESS MITTS

✳ ✳ ✳ ✳ INTERMEDIATE 2

It's amazing how a little bit of soft wool hugging your wrists and hands can raise your coziness meter several degrees, even if your fingers are open to the cold! Fingerless mitts are incredibly practical, and patterned ones bring just the right pop of color to a plain winter coat or sweater. They are also a great way to bridge seasons. These long fingerless mitts are knit in the round, except for the portion around the thumb opening. Switch around the colors and you could easily knit three pairs of mitts with three skeins of yarn. Ingrid Fingerless Mitts are a perfect place to practice purling in colorwork. There're only a few rows, and you'll catch on quickly.

SKILLS YOU'LL PRACTICE

DPN work. Long-tail cast on (page 184). Joining in the round seamlessly (page 37). Working 1x1 ribbing (k1, p1). Knitting and purling in two colors in the round, left and right together (pages 41–42 and 123–124). Reading a chart in both directions (page 9). Weaving a new color in (and out) (pages 38–39 and 44–45). Catching floats (pages 85–87). Crochet edge (page 185). Binding off (page 182).

BEGINNER TIP: Colorwork charts are read from right to left while you're knitting and left to right when you purl.

SIZES

WOMEN'S FINGERLESS MITT: One size fits most

MATERIALS

YARN: Worsted | Fleece and Harmony Selkirk Worsted | 100% Prince Edward Island 2-ply Wool | 200 yards (183 m) per 2.8-ounce (80-g) skein

MAIN COLOR (MC): Natural | 1 skein [117 yards (107 m)]

CONTRASTING COLOR 1 (CC1): Rhubarb | 1 skein [22 yards (20 m)]

CONTRASTING COLOR 2 (CC2): Ferry | 1 skein [38 yards (35 m)]

NEEDLES: One pair FlexiFlips or double-pointed needles (DPNS) to obtain the correct gauge

SUGGESTED NEEDLE SIZE: US 5 (3.75 mm) for colorwork

One pair of FlexiFlips or double-pointed needles one size smaller than gauge-size needles

SUGGESTED NEEDLE SIZE: US 4 (3.5 mm)

ADDITIONAL MATERIALS

Stitch marker, scissors, tapestry needle, and size G (4 mm) crochet hook for thumb edge

GAUGE AND SWATCH

24 stitches and 27 rounds/rows = 4 inches (10 cm)

FINISHED MEASUREMENTS

4 inches (10 cm) wide and 10 inches (25 cm) long

INSTRUCTIONS

1. CAST ON RIGHT-HAND MITT

With smaller needles and the MC, using a long-tail cast on, cast on 48 stitches.

2. RIBBING

Join for knitting in the round by knitting from the last stitch of the cast-on row to the first stitch of the cast-on row. Be careful not to twist the cast-on stitches. Round 1: *Knit 1, purl 1.* Repeat from * to * all the way around. Work the first 2 stitches with the working yarn and the tail from the long-tail cast on for a seamless join. (See the tutorial on page 37.) Place a marker at the beginning of the round. Work 1x1 ribbing for three rounds. Continue to work ribbing. On the last round, stop knitting 7 stitches before the marker.

3. BEGIN COLORWORK

On the last 7 stitches, weave in the CC1 in preparation for working in colorwork. Slip marker and change to larger needles for the colorwork portion. Begin on Stitch 1 of Row 4 on the chart (page 172). Read the chart from right to left, bottom to top (starting on Row 4). Knit Rounds 4–14. Catch floats where necessary. Carry the CC1 in your left hand and the MC in your right hand. This is so the pattern yarn is in the dominant position. If you are carrying the yarn in one hand, carry the CC to the left of the MC. Whichever method you use to knit with two colors, be consistent throughout the entire mitt. Seven stitches before the end of Round 5, weave in the CC2 in preparation to knit with it on Round 6. Slip marker and knit with the CC2 and the MC and weave out the tail from the CC1 for at least 7 stitches. Cut the CC1 and continue working Rounds 6–14. Continue in this manner, weaving in the new contrasting color just before you need to knit with it, and weave out the tail of the old CC when you are finished with it. This will keep the back of your work tidy and save time weaving in ends when you are finished with the mitt. Continue to knit the chart two times more for a total of 39 rounds.

4. WORK MITT FLAT TO MAKE A THUMBHOLE

Work Rows 1–14 of the chart flat to create a thumbhole. The thumbhole is located between Stitch 48 and Stitch 1.

ROW 1: (RS) Knit across all stitches and work Row 1 in colorwork. Stop at the end of the row. Turn.

ROW 2: (WS) Purl all stitches for Row 2 in colorwork. Turn.

Continue to knit the odd rows, turn the work, and then purl the even rows. Pay attention to keep the pattern correct. Carry both yarns to the edge of the mitt by catching the color you are not knitting with on the second-to-last stitch of each row. A simple way to catch the float on the purl side is to twist the CC2 around the MC.

5. CONTINUE KNITTING THE MITT IN THE ROUND

Join the last stitch of Row 14 to the first stitch of Round 1. Work Rounds 1–8 of the chart in the round.

6. HOMESTRETCH

Break the CC2. With smaller needles, knit one round with the MC only and weave out the tail from the CC2. Knit three rounds of 1x1 ribbing (k1, p1). Bind off all stitches, continuing 1x1 ribbing and decreasing 8 stitches evenly spaced while binding off. (Hint: Work *k1, p1, k1, p1, then ssk.* Repeat from * to * eight times.) Break yarn, leaving an 8-inch (20-cm) tail. Thread the tail of the yarn onto a tapestry needle. With a duplicate stitch, connect the last stitch of the round to the first stitch of the round.

7. PICK UP AND CROCHET THUMB EDGE

With a size G (4 mm) crochet hook and the MC, pick up and crochet one round of single crochet (22 stitches) around the thumbhole. Break the yarn and thread it onto a tapestry needle. Make a duplicate stitch to connect the end of the crochet round to the first crochet stitch in order to make the crochet round seamless around the thumb. Weave in the ends on the wrong side.

8. KNIT SECOND MITT

The left and right mitts are the same, so just make a second mitt.

9. FINISHING

Weave in ends. Steam block. Wear immediately or give them away to share the coziness.

INGRID SCHEMATIC

A- Circumference: 8 inches (20 cm)

B- Length: 10 inches (25 cm)

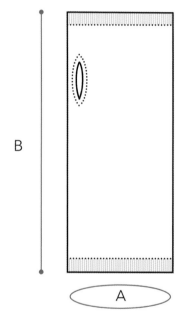

INGRID CHART

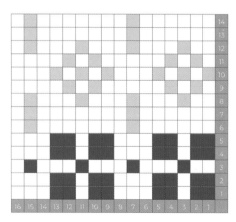

KEY

☐ = Main Color (MC)

■ = Contrasting Color 1 (CC1)

▨ = Contrasting Color 2 (CC2)

KRISTIANIA SWEATER

✳ ✳ ✳ ✳ INTERMEDIATE 2

When I was little, I used to love looking at old family photos with my grandma Hansen. They were beautiful black-and-white photos of loved ones from a different time and place. My favorite photo was of my great-grandpa Olsen as a toddler in Norway. On the back of the photo, there was a letter-pressed stamp with the name of the photo studio and the name of a town: Kristiania. Kristiania sounded like a fairytale to me. Grandpa Olsen was born and was a child there. Records show he emigrated from Kristiania to America. I always imagined Kristiania looked just like the castle on the sea that he used to paint and was forever intrigued by that gold-embossed stamp of a town that no longer exists. My grandfather was born during the late nineteenth century Norwegian romantic period— characterized by nostalgic art, music, and literature that celebrated nature, folklore, and Norwegian identity. Norway was a new country, so he brought his national pride with him to the New World. And his love for Norway was passed on to me. I named this sweater for my family's hometown that every Norwegian knows changed its name to Oslo in 1925. This sweater is only about 5 percent actual colorwork. But that 5 percent makes it feel 110 percent Nordic. It's easy for me to imagine my grandpa Olsen wearing this sweater as he crossed the Atlantic, dreaming of a new home yet still longing for the one he left behind.

SKILLS YOU'LL PRACTICE

Long-tail cast on (page 184). Splicing yarn (page 186). Joining in the round seamlessly (page 37). Working 1x1 ribbing (k1, p1). Knitting in the round. Stockinette stitch. Knitting and purling in two colors, left and right hands together (pages 41–42 and 123–124). Reading a chart (page 9). K2tog decrease (page 184). Ssk decrease (page 186). Three-needle bind off (page 187). Picking up stitches (page 186). Binding off (page 182). DPN work.

SIZES

XS (S, M, L, XL, 2XL, 3XL)

3–5 inches (7.5–12.75 cm) positive ease

MATERIALS

YARN: Worsted | Brooklyn Tweed Shelter | 100% American Targhee-Columbia Wool | 140 yards (128 m) per 1.75-ounce (50-g) skein

MAIN COLOR (MC): Fossil | 6 (7, 7, 8, 9, 10, 11) skeins [840 (900, 980, 1080, 1200, 1350, 1490) yards] / [768 (822, 896, 987, 1097, 1234, 1362) m]

CONTRASTING COLOR (CC): Charcoal | 1 skein [77 (85, 91, 101, 109, 117, 131) yards] / [71 (78, 83, 92, 100, 107, 120) m]

NEEDLES: One 32 (32, 40, 40, 40, 40, 40)-inch [80 (80, 100, 100, 100, 100, 100)-cm] circular needle for the body and a 16-inch (40-cm) circular needle for the sleeves in size needed to obtain gauge in colorwork and single color

SUGGESTED NEEDLE SIZE: US 8 (5 mm)

One 32 (32, 40, 40, 40, 40, 40)-inch [80 (80, 100, 100, 100, 100, 100)-cm] circular needle one size smaller than gauge-size needle for ribbing on body and a pair of double-pointed needles (DPNs) or FlexiFlips to use for 1x1 ribbing on the sleeves

SUGGESTED NEEDLE SIZE: US 7 (4.5 mm)

ADDITIONAL MATERIALS

Stitch markers, measuring tape, scissors, tapestry needle, sewing needle, fingering-weight yarn for sewing, and 1–2 pairs of Nordic clasps

GAUGE AND SWATCH

18 stitches and 24 rounds = 4 inches (10 cm)

Please swatch in the round to determine needle size.

FINISHED MEASUREMENTS

CHEST: 34¼ (37¾, 40½, 45, 48½, 52, 58¼) inches [87 (96, 103, 114.5, 123, 132, 148) cm]

SLEEVE LENGTH: 18 (18, 18, 19, 20, 23, 23) inches [46 (46, 46, 48.5, 51, 58.5, 58.5) cm]

BODY LENGTH: 15½ (16, 16, 16½, 17½, 18½, 18½) inches [39 (41, 41, 42, 44.5, 47, 47) cm]

3–5 inches (7.5–12.75 cm) positive ease

INSTRUCTIONS

1. CAST ON

With smaller needles, and MC, using a long-tail cast on, cast on 154 (170, 182, 202, 218, 234, 262) stitches.

2. RIBBING

Place a marker at the beginning of the round. The beginning of the round is on the left side of the sweater. Join for knitting in the round by knitting from the last stitch of the cast-on row to the first stitch of the cast-on row. Be careful not to twist the cast-on stitches. Round 1: *Knit 1, purl 1.* Repeat from * to * all the way around. Work 1x1 ribbing until the sweater measures 2 (2, 2, 2½, 2½, 3, 3) inches [5 (5, 5, 6.5, 6.5, 7.5, 7.5) cm].

3. KNIT BODY

Knit onto the larger needles and knit in the round until the body measures 15½ (16, 16, 16½, 17½, 18½, 18½) inches [39 (41, 41, 42, 44.5, 47, 47) cm] or 7½ (8, 8½, 9, 9½, 10, 10½) inches [19 (20, 21.5, 23, 24, 25.5, 26.5) cm] shorter than the desired length for the sweater.

4. SPLIT BACK AND FRONT AND KNIT BACK OF SWEATER

Knit across 77 (85, 91, 101, 109, 117, 131) front stitches and place them onto a holder.

Knit across 77 (85, 91, 101, 109, 117, 131) back stitches.

Turn and work flat in stockinette until the back of the sweater measures 20 (21, 21½, 22½, 24, 25½, 26) inches [51 (53.5, 54.75, 57, 61, 64.75, 66) cm] or 3 inches (7.5 cm) from the desired length and after completing a WS row. Turn.

5. WORK COLORWORK LOCATED AT THE TOP OF THE BACK OF THE SWEATER

With the RS facing, beginning on Stitch 7 (3, 8, 3, 7, 3, 4) and ending on Stitch 3 (7, 2, 7, 3, 7, 6), knit colorwork Chart 1 (page 181) for sixteen rows in stockinette.

ROW 1: (RS) Knit in colorwork.

ROW 2: (WS) Leave the MC behind and purl with the CC. Slide work from the right needle along the cable to the left needle.

ROW 3: (WS again) Purl with the MC.

ROWS 4–9: Work colorwork in stockinette.

ROW 10: (RS) Leave the CC behind and knit with the MC. Slide work from the right needle along the cable to the left needle.

ROW 11: (RS again) Knit with the CC.

ROWS 12–15: Work colorwork in stockinette.

ROW 16: Purl with the MC.

Sweater measures 23 (24, 24½, 25½, 27, 28½, 29) inches [58 (61, 62.5, 64.75, 68.5, 72, 73.5) cm] or your desired length.

Place 24 (28, 30, 34, 36, 39, 44) right back shoulder stitches onto a holder. Place 24 (28, 30, 34, 36, 39, 44) left back shoulder stitches onto a holder. Place center 29 (29, 31, 33, 37, 39, 43) stitches onto a holder for the neckband. Set aside.

6. KNIT FRONT OF SWEATER

With RS facing and the MC, knit across the front of the sweater. Turn. Work flat in stockinette for 1 inch (2.5 cm). Finish after completing a WS row. Turn.

7. SEPARATE THE LEFT FRONT FROM THE RIGHT FRONT OF THE SWEATER

With RS facing, knit across 38 (42, 45, 50, 54, 58, 65) stitches and bind off one stitch for the center neck stitch. Note that the second stitch of the bind off is the first stitch on the right front of the sweater. Knit stitches for the right front. There is a total of 38 (42, 45, 50, 54, 58, 65) stitches each for the right and left front of the sweater. Place the left front stitches onto a holder.

8. WORK RIGHT FRONT STITCHES

Work in stockinette until right front measures 19¼ (20¼, 20¾, 21¾, 23¼, 24¾, 25¼) inches [49 (51.5, 52.75, 55.25, 59, 63, 64) cm] or 3¾ inches (9.5 cm) less than the desired length and after completing a WS row. Turn.

9. SHAPE NECK AND WORK COLORWORK FROM CHART 1

Continue working flat and shape the neckline. Colorwork starts on Row 5 of neck shaping. Establish colorwork pattern and keep pattern correct, even with binding off at the neckline. Hints are given to keep you lined up. Work rows carefully following line-by-line instructions. The front of the sweater is worked in stockinette. Occasionally two rows will be purled or knit consecutively in order to knit with one color at a time and to have both colors on the same side when you need two strands for colorwork. Work with only the stitches for one side at a time on circular needles so that you can knit or purl two rows consecutively.

ROW 1: (RS) With the MC, bind off the first 6 (6, 7, 8, 10, 11, 13) stitches. Knit to the end of the row. Turn. Total stitches: 32 (36, 38, 42, 44, 47, 52).

ROW 2: (WS) With the MC, purl one row. Turn.

ROW 3: (RS) With the MC, bind off the first 3 stitches and knit to the end of the row. Turn. Total stitches: 29 (33, 35, 39, 41, 44, 49).

ROW 4: (WS) With the MC, purl one row. Turn.

ROW 5: (RS) Bind off 2 stitches at the neck edge and begin colorwork starting on Stitch 1 (1, 2, 3, 5, 6, 8) of Row 1 on Chart 1 and ending on Stitch 3 (7, 2, 7, 3, 7, 6) of Chart 1. Turn. Total stitches: 27 (31, 33, 37, 39, 42, 47). (Hint: On Row 5, two stitches are bound off at the neck's edge and the colorwork begins with the first stitch after the bind off [or rather in the middle of binding off the second stitch]. In order to bind off two stitches, three stitches are worked. To accomplish this feat, work the bind off in this manner: Knit 2 stitches in the MC. Bind off the first stitch over the second stitch. Begin the colorwork on the third stitch, starting with Stitch 1 [1, 2, 3, 5, 6, 8] of Chart 1. Bind off the second stitch over the third stitch [the colorwork stitch]. Now you have bound off 2 stitches at the neck's edge, and the colorwork begins after the first two stitches have been bound off. Congratulations! You did it!)

ROW 6: (WS) Leave the MC behind and, with the CC, purl Row 2 of Chart 1.

ROW 7: (WS again) With the MC, purl Row 3 of Chart 1. Turn.

ROW 8: (RS) Bind off one stitch at the neck's edge. (Hint: Bind off Stitch 1 [1, 2, 3, 5, 6, 8] and continue in pattern to knit Row 4 of Chart 1.) Turn. Total stitches: 26 (30, 32, 36, 38, 41, 46).

ROW 9: (WS) Purl and work Row 5 of Chart 1 starting with Stitch 3 (7, 2, 7, 3, 7, 6). Read the chart from left to right. Turn.

ROW 10: (RS) Bind off one stitch at the neck's edge and knit Row 6 of Chart 1. (Hint: Bind off Stitch 2 [2, 3, 4, 6, 7, 1].) Turn. Total stitches: 25 (29, 31, 35, 37, 40, 45).

ROW 11: (WS) Purl Row 7 of Chart 1 in colorwork beginning with Stitch 3 (7, 2, 7, 3, 7, 6). Read the chart from left to right. Turn.

ROW 12: (RS) Bind off one stitch at the neck's edge (Hint: Bind off Stitch 3 [3, 4, 5, 7, 8, 2].) and continue in pattern. Work Row 8 of Chart 1 in colorwork. Turn. Total stitches: 24 (28, 30, 34, 36, 39, 44).

ROW 13: (WS) Purl Row 9 in colorwork, starting with Stitch 3 (7, 2, 7, 3, 7, 6). Turn.

NOTE: Total neck decrease over thirteen rows is 14 (14, 15, 16, 18, 19, 21) stitches.

ROW 14: (RS) With the MC, knit Row 10 on the chart.

ROW 15: (RS again) With the CC, knit Row 11. Turn.

ROW 16: (WS) Purl Row 12 in colorwork beginning with Stitch 3 (7, 2, 7, 3, 7, 6). Turn.

ROW 17: (RS) Knit Row 13 in colorwork beginning with Stitch 4 (4, 5, 6, 8, 1, 3). Turn.

ROW 18: (WS) Purl Row 14 in colorwork beginning with Stitch 3 (7, 2, 7, 3, 7, 6). Turn.

ROW 19: (RS) Knit Row 15 in colorwork beginning with Stitch 4 (4, 5, 6, 8, 1, 3). Turn.

ROW 20: (WS) With the MC, purl Row 16.

Place 24 (28, 30, 34, 36, 39, 44) right front stitches onto a holder.

10. WORK LEFT FRONT STITCHES AFTER SPLIT

Work in stockinette until left front measures 19¼ (20¼, 20¾, 21¾, 23¼, 24¾, 25¼) inches [49 (51.5, 52.75, 55.25, 59, 63, 64) cm] or 3¾ inches (9.5 cm) less than the desired length and after completing a RS row. Turn.

11. SHAPE LEFT NECK AND WORK COLORWORK FROM CHART 1

ROW 1: (WS) Purl in the MC, bind off 6 (6, 7, 8, 10, 11, 13) stitches and purl to the end of the row. Turn. Total stitches: 32 (36, 38, 42, 44, 47, 52).

ROW 2: (RS) Knit one row. Turn.

ROW 3: (WS) With the MC, bind off the first 3 stitches and purl to the end of the row. Turn. Total stitches: 29 (33, 35, 39, 41, 44, 49).

ROW 4: (RS) With the MC, knit one row. Turn.

ROW 5: (WS) With the MC, bind off 2 stitches at the neck's edge and begin working colorwork on Row 1 of Chart 1, reading from left to right on the chart beginning on Stitch 1 (1, 8, 7, 5, 4, 2) and ending on Stitch 7 (3, 8, 3, 7, 3, 4). Turn. Total stitches: 27 (31, 33, 37, 39, 42, 47). See hint for binding off 2 stitches and beginning colorwork at the same time on page 177.

ROW 6: (RS) Leaving the MC behind, knit with the CC only on Row 2 of Chart 1.

ROW 7: (RS again) With the MC, knit Row 3 of Chart 1. Now both colors of yarn are ready to work in colorwork. Turn.

ROW 8: (WS) Bind off one stitch at the neck's edge. (Hint: Bind off Stitch 1 [1, 8, 7, 5, 4, 2].) Continue in pattern to knit Row 4 in colorwork. Turn. Total stitches: 26 (30, 32, 36, 38, 41, 46).

ROW 9: (RS) Knit and work Row 5 in colorwork, beginning on Stitch 7 (3, 8, 3, 7, 3, 4), reading the chart from right to left. Turn.

ROW 10: (WS) Bind off one stitch at the neck's edge and purl Row 6 of Chart 1. (Hint: Bind off Stitch 8 [8, 7, 6, 4, 3, 1].) Turn. Total stitches: 25 (29, 31, 35, 37, 40, 45).

ROW 11: (RS) Knit Row 7 in colorwork beginning on Stitch 7 (3, 8, 3, 7, 3 4). Turn.

ROW 12: (WS) Bind off one stitch at the neck's edge and purl Row 8 in colorwork. (Hint: Bind off Stitch 7 [7, 6, 5, 3, 2, 8].) Turn. Total stitches: 24 (28, 30, 34, 36, 39, 44).

ROW 13: (RS) Knit Row 9 in colorwork. Turn.

> **NOTE:** Total neck decrease over thirteen rows is 14 (14, 15, 16, 18, 19, 21) stitches.

Complete Rows 10–16 of Chart 1 in stockinette.

ROW 14: (WS) With the MC, purl Row 10.

ROW 15: (WS again) With the CC, purl Row 11. Turn.

ROW 16: (RS) Knit Row 12 in colorwork, starting with Stitch 7 (3, 8, 3, 7, 3, 4). Turn.

ROW 17: (WS) Purl Row 13 in colorwork, starting with Stitch 6 (6, 5, 4, 2, 1, 7). Turn.

ROW 18: (RS) Knit Row 14 in colorwork, starting with Stitch 7 (3, 8, 3, 7, 3, 4). Turn.

ROW 19: (WS) Purl Row 15 in colorwork, starting with Stitch 6 (6, 5, 4, 2, 1, 7). Turn.

ROW 20: (RS) With the MC, knit Row 16.

Place left front 24 (28, 30, 34, 36, 39, 44) stitches onto a holder.

12. JOIN SHOULDER SEAMS

Place 24 (28, 30, 34, 36, 39, 44) stitches for right back onto a DPN and 24 (28, 30, 34, 36, 39, 44) stitches for right front onto another DPN. With right sides facing, join shoulders with a three-needle bind off.

Repeat for the left side.

13. PICK UP AND KNIT SLEEVE

Starting at the right underarm, pick up and knit 60 (64, 68, 72, 76, 80, 84) stitches around the right armhole for the right sleeve. Place a marker at the underarm to mark the beginning of the round. Knit one round. Beginning on Stitch 1 of Chart 2 (page 181), knit Rounds 1–9 in colorwork.

With the MC, knit for 1 inch (2.5 cm).

WORK DECREASE ROUND: K1, k2tog, knit to 3 stitches before marker, ssk, k1 (2 stitches decreased).

Knit seven rounds.

WORK DECREASE ROUND: K1, k2tog, knit to 3 stitches before marker, ssk, k1 (2 stitches decreased).

Continue working a decrease round every 7 (7, 7, 6, 6, 6, 6) rounds of knitting until you have 40 (42, 42, 44, 46, 48, 50) stitches. Total of 10 (11, 13, 14, 15, 16, 17) decrease rounds. Continue to knit sleeve until the sleeve measures 16 (16, 16, 17, 18, 21, 21) inches [40.5 (40.5, 40.5, 43, 46, 53, 53) cm] or 2 inches (5 cm) shorter than desired sleeve length. You can try on Kristiania to tailor the sleeve length.

Switch to smaller DPNs and work 1x1 ribbing (k1, p1) for 2 inches (5 cm).

14. KNIT SECOND SLEEVE

Repeat Step 13 and knit the second sleeve.

15. WORK NECKBAND

With RS facing, using smaller circular needles and MC, pick up approximately 24 (25, 26, 27, 28, 29, 30) stitches along the right front neckline and pick up and knit one stitch at the top of the shoulder. Knit 29 (29, 31, 33, 37, 39, 43) stitches across the back stitches on the holder and pick up and knit one stitch at the top of the shoulder. Pick up and knit 24 (25, 26, 27, 28, 29, 30) stitches down the left front. Total stitches: 79 (81, 85, 89, 95, 99, 105). Work Chart 3 (page 181) in stockinette. The neckband begins and ends on Stitch 1.

ROW 1: (WS) Purl with the CC, starting on Stitch 1 of Row 1 of Chart 3. Turn.

ROW 2: (RS) With the CC and the MC, knit in colorwork, beginning with Stitch 1 of Row 2 on Chart 3. End on Stitch 1. Turn.

ROW 3: (WS) Purl Row 3 in colorwork. Turn.

ROW 4: (RS) Leave the MC behind and, with the CC, knit Row 4 of Chart 3.

ROW 5: (RS again) Knit with the MC. Break the CC and weave in the tail. Turn.

ROW 6: (WS) With the MC, knit for turning row. Turn.

ROWS 7–12: Continuing with the MC, work in stockinette for five rows.

ROW 13: Bind off all stitches. Keep tension even and consistent with gauge. Break the yarn and leave a long tail to use for sewing.

Fold neckband and, using the tail, sew neckband down to the inside of the sweater with a whipstitch.

16. WORK FRONT BANDS

Starting at the bottom of the right front opening, using the smaller needles and the CC, pick up and knit stitches along the front band edge. Pick up 3 stitches for every four knit rows from the bottom of the front band to the top of the neckband. Turn. With WS facing, purl one row. Turn. With RS facing, purl one row for a folding row. Turn. With WS facing, purl and work in stockinette for four rows. Bind off all stitches. Fold the band and, using the tail, sew the band down to the inside of the sweater with a whipstitch. Fasten the short side of the band to the center bound-off stitch that separates the left side from the right side with a mattress stitch.

Pick up and work the left side in the same manner, but start at the top of the neckband edge.

17. SEW ON CLASPS

Sew the clasps, centered on the neckband. Sew the hook on the right side, and the eye on the left side.

If using a second pair of clasps, center the second pair in the center of the front bands.

18. FINISHING

Weave in all the remaining ends. Steam block. Enjoy!

KRISTIANIA CHART 1

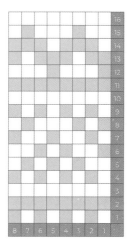

KRISTIANIA CHART 2

KRISTIANIA CHART 3

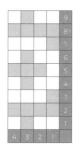

KEY

⬜ = Main Color (MC)

🟩 = Contrasting Color (CC)

KRISTIANIA SCHEMATIC

A- Chest circumference: 34¼ (37¾, 40½, 45, 48½, 52, 58¼) inches [87 (96, 103, 114.5, 123, 132, 148) cm]

B- Body length to underarm: 15½ (16, 16, 16½, 17½, 18½, 18½) inches [39 (41, 41, 42, 44.5, 47, 47) cm]

C- Arms/sleeve depth: 7½ (8, 8½, 9, 9½, 10, 10½) inches [19 (20.5, 21.5, 22.75, 24, 25.5, 26.75) cm]

D- Front slit: 3½ (4, 4½, 5, 5½, 6, 6½) inches [9 (10, 11.5, 12.75, 14, 15.25, 16.5) cm]

E- Sleeve length: 18 (18, 18, 19, 20, 23, 23) inches [46 (46, 46, 48.5, 51, 58.5, 58.5) cm]

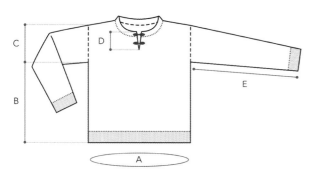

BASIC KNITTING TECHNIQUES

BACKWARD LOOP INCREASE

It's simply a loop with a twist, and it makes a new stitch. This is my favorite increase! It's the perfect invisible increase for colorwork. It's a secret weapon.

BINDING OFF

Binding off is a two-stitch process. Knit one stitch, knit a second stitch, then, with the left needle, pull the first stitch over the second stitch, binding off the first stitch. Then knit a third stitch and, with the left needle, pull the second stitch over the third stitch. Continue until all the required stitches are bound off.

This is a basic skill, but let me remind you to bind off at the same gauge as you knit. Be consistent here. Binding off too tightly makes neckbands too tight, and binding off too loosely makes neckbands sloppy.

BUTTONHOLES

To make a simple buttonhole, I like to bind off three stitches on the row for the buttonhole, and then on the next row, cast on three stitches right above the bound-off stitches. Simple. Reinforce the buttonhole with a buttonhole stitch.

1.

Backward Loop Increase: Twist the yarn around your left thumb.

2.

Right needle enters up through the backward loop at the top of the X.

3.

Place loop on your right needle.

4.

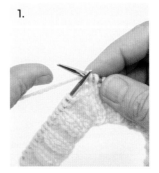

Pull gently so that the tension is consistent.

CATCHING FLOATS

See the tutorials included in the Linnea Pullover in Chapter 3 (pages 85–87).

1) Guidelines for catching floats (page 85)

2) Catching floats with the contrasting color (page 86)

3) Catching floats with the main color (page 87)

DPNS (AKA DOUBLE-POINTED NEEDLES)

They come in packs of 5 needles. They are used for working small circumferences. Divide the stitches evenly among 4 needles. The 4 needles make a circle (technically a square). Interlock the tips of the needles together to make the circle stronger. The fifth needle is a working needle. Wood needles are easiest for first-time DPN knitters. I love the clicking sound that DPNs make.

DUPLICATE STITCH

See the tutorial in the embroidery section of the Swedish Lovikka Mittens in Chapter 2 (page 55). The duplicate stitch is a powerful tool to use in colorwork. You can use it to add color to a finished project, like in the Swedish Lovikka Mittens, or to add a third color, like in the Greta Pullover in Chapter 3 (page 107). You can also use it to correct small mistakes in colorwork by embroidering the correct color over the mis-knit stitch. Beyond colorwork, the duplicate stitch can be used to connect the last stitch of a neckband to the first stitch in the neckband, creating an endless circle. You will find many uses for this valuable trompe l'oeil.

DUPLICATE STITCH JOIN

This is one of the secrets to beautifully finished garments that are knit in the round. When you finish binding off, break the yarn and use the tail to join the last stitch of the bind off to the first stitch of the bind-off row. Follow the embroidery tutorial for the duplicate stitch on page 55 and make a new horizontal stitch to bridge the gap from the end of the round to the beginning of the round and make the top of your sweaters (or slippers) into seamless rounds. This is a fabulous trick!

FRENCH KNOT

See the tutorial in the embroidery section of the Swedish Lovikka Mittens in Chapter 2 (pages 53–54).

JOINING IN THE ROUND SEAMLESSLY

Join by knitting the first two stitches with the working yarn and the tail from the long-tail cast on. Make sure that on the next row, you treat the stitches with the working yarn and the long-tail cast on as one stitch. You are going to love this join! It does away with the gap that often happens when joining to knit in the round. See the tutorial on page 37.

KITCHENER STITCH

The Kitchener stitch basically creates a row of knitting using a tapestry needle threaded with a strand of yarn to connect two rows of live stitches. I usually use this stitch to graft the underarm stitches together. There are a lot of steps used in this technique. Place the underarm stitches for the body onto a DPN (this is the front needle). Place the underarm stitches for the sleeve on a DPN (this is the back needle). Using a tapestry needle threaded with the yarn used in the sweater, thread the needle from the front stitches to the back stitches, grafting them together. Here is a cheat sheet to help you remember how it's done. Before you begin, you'll need a definition of a couple of terms: "purl front on" means to insert the tapestry needle into the front stitch as to purl, keeping the stitch on the needle. "Knit back off" means to insert the tapestry needle into the back needle as to knit and to slip the stitch off the needle.

HERE'S THE CHEAT SHEET.

Set up the first two stitches: Purl front on, knit back on, then *knit front off, purl front on, purl back off, knit back on.* Repeat from * to * until the last stitch, then knit front off, purl back off.

See the video tutorial at Scandiwork.com until you get the hang of it.

And a really helpful tip is to leave an 8-inch (20-cm) tail at the beginning and end of the Kitchener stitch. Turn the sweater inside out and use the tails to connect the stitches that are grafted together for the underarm to the body with a mattress stitch to close up any holes.

K2TOG DECREASE

This decrease makes a right-leaning decrease. The decrease is worked by literally knitting the second stitch together with the first stitch, and, in the process, the first stitch is pulled under the second stitch, making the second stitch the only stitch you will be able to see. This is important to know in colorwork. Use k2tog when the first stitch is in the main color and the second stitch is in the contrasting color so you can see the colorwork stitch.

KNITTING WITH TWO COLORS, LEFT AND RIGHT TOGETHER

See the colorwork tutorials included in the Sander Cowl in Chapter 2 (pages 41–42).

KNITTING WITH YARN IN YOUR LEFT HAND

See the tutorials included in Chapter 1 (page 19).

1) Setting up for left-handed knitting (page 22)

2) Left-handed knitting (page 23)

3) Left-handed purling (page 24)

KNITTING WITH YARN IN YOUR RIGHT HAND

See the tutorials included in Chapter 1 (page 19).

1) Setting up for right-handed knitting (page 25)

2) Right-handed knitting (page 26)

3) Right-handed purling (page 27)

LAZY DAISY STITCH

See the tutorial in the embroidery section of the Swedish Lovikka Mittens pattern in Chapter 2 (page 52).

LONG-TAIL CAST ON

This is my favorite cast on. I use this in every project in the book. It's a beautiful start for any project. The trick is casting on firmly and evenly but not too tightly or loosely. Aim for the perfect amount of tension. Don't cast on loosely to make knitting the first row easier. That easy row to knit is not worth having bedraggled ribbing. The cast on needs to match the tension for the rest of the knit. A beautiful cast on sets the tone for the project. Don't be sloppy here. And never use a slipknot when you begin the long-tail cast on. If you do, that knot will always be at the bottom of your project. See the tutorial for a two-color long-tail cast on in the Stjerne Slippers pattern in Chapter 4 (pages 126–127). For a single-color long-tail cast on, the long tail goes over your thumb, and the yarn from the skein goes over your index finger.

MAKING A CROCHET EDGE

A simple crochet edge is used on the Olsen Slippers (page 143) and Ingrid Fingerless Mitts (page 169) in Chapter 4. Work a single crochet along the edge of the garment in this manner:

1. Insert the crochet hook into the center of the knit stitch on the edge.

2. Grab the yarn being held on your left index finger and draw the loop through the center of the knit stitch on the edge (1 loop on hook).

3. Then, with the crochet hook, reach over the edge and grab the working yarn from your left index finger and draw the loop through the loop on the hook to complete the stitch.

Repeat working under and over the edge to enclose the edge of the slipper (or thumbholes on the mitts) with a chain stitch.

MAKING A PICOT EDGE

This lovely edge is incorporated into the Liv Mitts in Chapter 1 (page 29). It's made by knitting into the front and knitting into the back of the last stitch.

ROW 1: Knit to the last stitch and knit into the front and the back of the last stitch.

ROW 2: Knit across the row.

ROW 3: Knit to the last stitch and knit into the front and the back of the last stitch.

ROW 4: Bind off the first two stitches and knit to the end of the row.

MATTRESS STITCH

This is a beautiful way to sew seams together. I use this technique in the Liv Mitts pattern in Chapter 1 (page 29) and to graft underarms together in yoke sweaters when the underarm stitches are bound off. This is one of my favorite tricks for beautiful seams. Repeat these four steps to sew a seam together with the right sides facing out.

Mattress stitch: Right sides facing, insert the tapestry needle under two strands of yarn on the left side.

Pull stitch gently to bring the two sides together.

Insert the tapestry needle under two strands of yarn on the right side.

Pull gently to bring the two sides together. This puts the seam on the inside of the mitt.

PICKING UP STITCHES

When picking up stitches, simply knit into the row below to create a new, seamless row. Whenever you are picking up stitches vertically for a neckband or picking up stitches for a sleeve, you need to match your stitch gauge to the row gauge. The standard for worsted weight yarn is approximately three stitches for every four rows. The standard for DK weight is pick up five stitches for every six rows. The number of stitches may vary depending on your row gauge. If your row gauge matches your stitch gauge exactly, then you will pick up stitch for stitch. Make adjustments as necessary to match your individual knitting. Pick up enough stitches to make the work look great and to lay flat. Use your best judgment here and don't pick up a stitch if it makes a hole. Take your time and be picky.

PURLING WITH TWO COLORS, LEFT AND RIGHT TOGETHER

See the colorwork tutorials included in the Stjerne Slippers pattern in Chapter 4 (pages 123–124).

READING A CHART

See the "Following Charts" section of the Introduction (page 9).

RUNNING BACKSTITCH

I use this hand-sewing technique when sewing together the heels of my slippers. I like the running back stitch because it makes the stitches close together so that there are no holes or gaps in the seams. With the right sides of the heels facing, insert the needle down through the fabric, about ⅛ inch (0.25 cm) to the right, then bring the needle up about ¼ inch (0.5 cm) to the right of where you started. Repeat, sewing the fabric together with loops that overlap.

SL1-K2TOG-PSSO DECREASE

This stitch decreases two stitches at once. You slip the first stitch, then knit the next two stitches together, and then pass the slipped stitch over the stitch that was used to knit two stitches together. I use this in the Freja Hat in Chapter 2 (page 75). All the decreases happen between the star motifs. Remember to start the decrease on the last stitch of the row before the decrease row.

SPLICING YARN

Remember that there are no knots in knitting. Splicing is the best way to join one skein to the next. Simply fray the end of the old skein and fray the end of the new skein. Overlap the frayed end with a solid part of yarn on the other skein. Moisten the join with spit—sorry, but it works—and rub the ends together between the palms of your hands, like you are making a snake with play dough. Basically, you are spinning the old yarn and the new yarn together. Make sure you make the splice the same width as the yarn so that you can't see where the old yarn stops and the new yarn begins. Make sure your hands are clean! Be extra careful with light-colored yarns. If you are working with yarn with multiple plies, you can thin out a single ply to help you achieve the perfect width in your splice.

SSK DECREASE

Slip the first stitch as to knit, slip the second stitch as to knit, and put your left needle into the front of both slipped stitches and knit them together. This is a left-leaning decrease that, in colorwork, makes the first stitch cover up the second stitch in the decrease. It is perfect to use this decrease when the first stitch is in the contrasting color and the second stitch is in either the main color or a contrasting color, and the pattern will still show.

THREE-NEEDLE BIND OFF

This is my favorite way to make a seam at the top of a shoulder. Try it on the Kristiania Sweater (page 173) and the Little Haakon Sweater (page 135) in Chapter 4. Place the right-front shoulder stitches on a DPN and the right-back shoulder stitches on another DPN. With the right sides of the fabric facing, join the first stitch from the front needle to the first stitch from the back needle by knitting them together. Join the second stitch from the front to the second stitch on the back by knitting them together and then bind off the first stitch over the second stitch. Continue in this manner to bind off all the stitches.

TVINNARAND STITCH

See the tutorial included in the Stjerne Slippers pattern in Chapter 4 (pages 130–131). I love this stitch. It's a Latvian braid with an extra twist. You can also practice tvinnarand on the Midsommar Pillow (page 159) and the Selbu Mittens (page 151).

TWO-COLOR LONG-TAIL CAST ON

See the tutorial included in the Stjerne Slippers pattern in Chapter 4 (pages 126–127). I use this trick for adding stitches for a steek, for the instep on my slippers, to cast on more stitches after making a thumbhole on a mitten, or when making a pocket. You have two strands of yarn ready to be used in a long-tail cast on. You may alternate the colors or cast on following a colorwork chart, whichever works best for your project. It's the perfect way to cast on more stitches in a field of colorwork.

WEAVING IN A NEW COLOR

See the tutorial included in the Sander Cowl pattern in Chapter 2 (pages 38–39). I love this trick. If you learn this skill, it will make a more beautiful inside of your knitting, the colorwork stitches will be more secure, the first stitch in the new color will be the same size as the rest of the colorwork stitches, and it will save you time by weaving in the ends as you go. The added bonus is that when you work colorwork with multiple colors, as in the Magnus Pullover in Chapter 2 (page 63), it will keep the back of your work tidy and eliminate the need to weave in lots of ends.

WEAVING OUT A NEW COLOR

See the tutorial included in the Sander Cowl pattern in Chapter 2 (pages 44–45). This time-saving step is basically the same as weaving in the new color and shares all the benefits. The only difference is how you begin and end the process. This step is a game changer. I've named it "weaving out a color" because I weave in the tail until the yarn runs out. I'm pretty sure I'm the only person in the world who calls this process weaving out. I like to think I've coined a phrase. Humor me.

RESOURCES

Working with beautiful yarn is essential for creating long-lasting heirloom knits. You can find all of the gorgeous yarn used for the projects in this book, as pictured, from the following yarn manufacturers.

BICHES ET BÛCHES
www.bichesetbuches.com
France

BROOKLYN TWEED
www.brooklyntweed.com
Portland, Oregon
USA

FLEECE AND HARMONY
www.fleeceandharmony.com
Belfast, Prince Edward Island
Canada

HARRISVILLE DESIGNS
www.harrisville.com
Harrisville, New Hampshire
USA

RAUMA
www.raumagarn.no
Norway

STUDIO DONEGAL
www.studiodonegal.ie
Ireland

WOOLFOLK
www.woolfolkyarn.com
Portland, Oregon
USA

ACKNOWLEDGMENTS

First of all, thank you to my mother and grandmother for teaching me to make things with my hands when I was small. Thanks for teaching me to make the inside of my work as pretty as the outside (a wonderful metaphor for life). Thanks for teaching me about the generation I never knew, seamlessly weaving their lives into mine. And above all, thank you for teaching me that making things is a way to show love. I felt your love in every quilt, handmade doll, and piece of clothing you made for me. Because of you, I know that hopes, dreams, protection, and love can be knit into every single row.

Thank you to my children, Dex, Anna, Xander, and Benji. Thanks for being the official models of Scandiwork (along with your spouses and children). Thanks for lifelong knitting requests that helped me grow as a knitter and designer. Thanks for caring if you were in line for the next sweater, and for your patience when you weren't. And thanks for knowing everything I ever made for you was a love note from me.

Thanks, Dex, for being my personal tech support and for remoting in anytime day or night to solve tech problems. Thanks, Paula, for measuring your children at a moment's notice and making time for us to photograph you and your beautiful children during a difficult time. Thanks, Anna, for helping me brainstorm projects, rework copy, plan photoshoots, and then modeling over (and over) when you would much rather have been holding beautiful baby Fritz. Thanks, Ben, for taking the early Scandiwork photos that led to this opportunity and for retouching every photo in this book. Thanks, Xander, for talking me into writing this book, modeling, checking on my progress daily, planning birthday parties, and dropping everything to help. Thanks, Ada, for working through prototypes to help me understand what makes a great hat, and for using your mad illustration skills to create the schematics. Thanks to Benji and Lizzy for traipsing along to multiple photo shoots across the Wasatch Front and for feeding us while we worked day and night to make deadlines. And thanks to all of you for helping us find joy in the journey. This book, like everything we do, has been a family project.

Thanks to all my knitting (and non-knitting) friends and students around the world. Thanks for your friendship, encouragement, feedback, advice, props, meals, and support. My life is better for knowing you.

To local yarn stores near and far: Thanks for the yarn, the teaching opportunities, the speedy deliveries, and keeping your small businesses going so we can see, touch, and feel yarn before we add it to our stash. Thanks to my local shops, Blazing Needles and Harmony Provo, and to my friends at Tolt and The Wooly Thistle farther afield. You are all my heroes.

To my friends at Biches et Bûches, Brooklyn Tweed, Fleece and Harmony, Harrisville Designs, Rauma, Studio Donegal, and Woolfolk: Thank you for making beautiful yarn for the world to knit with. Thank you for your generous yarn support. And thanks for getting yarn to me during a global pandemic. You're the best.

Thank you to my editor, Rebecca Fofonoff, my copy editor, Ashley Casteel, and the team at Page Street Publishing. Thanks for having the vision to publish a book for knitters who are new to colorwork and for asking me to write it. Thank you for your careful editing, thoughtful advice, and attention to detail.

Thanks to my talented tech editor, Heli Rajavaara. I appreciate your keen eye, your patience, and your ability to see the whole picture amidst the fine details. I'm so glad *Laine* magazine brought us together. It was worth sending my patterns back and forth to Finland to have you on my team.

Finally, to the love of my life, Chris Drysdale. Thank you for caring about this book as much as I do. Thanks for the brilliant photography. Thank you for being my in-house copy editor. Thanks for all the evenings and late nights after working your real job all day. Thanks for making meals, walking the dog, throwing family parties, and putting up with tables covered with yarn and sweaters all over the house for our entire married life. Thanks for making me laugh along the way. You are the center of my world.

ABOUT THE AUTHOR

KRISTIN DRYSDALE is an independent knitwear designer and instructor. She learned to knit while studying abroad and has been knitting ever since. She majored in German and European History at the University of Utah and studied at Christian-Albrecht Universität in Kiel, Germany, and Universität Salzburg in Austria. Inspired by her heritage, she specializes in Scandinavian colorwork and design. Her designs have been published in *Laine* magazine and *Knitter's Magazine*. She has also designed for Harrisville Designs and Brown Sheep Company and frequently self-publishes patterns. She teaches workshops across the United States and loves to share colorwork tips and tricks gleaned from a lifetime of Scandinavian knitting. Kristin is the founder of Scandiwork. You can see more of her work at Scandiwork.com. She lives in Salt Lake City, Utah, with her husband and Mr. Bingley, her dog. She has four married children and three grandchildren who live close enough for sleepovers and Sunday dinners. This is her first book.

INDEX

A

adventurous beginner projects
    Dagna Hat, 95–99
    Freja Hat, 75–79
    Lars Hat, 57–60
    Magnus Pullover, 63–67
    Maja Pullover, 69–74
    Sander Cowl, 35–46
    Setesdal Cowl, 91–94
    Swedish Lovikka Mittens, 47–55
Aittamaa, Erika, 47
Alpaca 50% Norwegian Wool, 79
American Cormo and Wool, 95
American Targhee Wool, 83, 101
American Targhee-Columbia
    Wool, 63, 69, 173

B

backward loop increase, 182
Barndoor, 122
beginner projects. *See also* adventurous beginner projects
    Liv Mitts, 29–30
Biches & Bûches Le Gros
    Lambswool, 107, 113, 135, 159
binding off, 182
Brooklyn Tweed Arbor, 83, 101
Brooklyn Tweed Shelter, 63, 69,
    173
buttonholes, 182

C

casting on, 12
catching floats
    1-stitch process, 87
    2-stitch process, 86
    colorwork and, 16, 81
    guidelines for, 85
    tip for, 159
charts
    following, 9, 186
    marking the row, 15
    memorizing the pattern, 14
    redrawing by hand, 15

    using knitting as, 15
    using visual relationships, 14–15
checkerboard pattern, 162
children's sweaters
    Little Greta Pullover, 113–117
    Little Haakon Sweater, 135–141
circular needles, 11, 176
colorwork
    casting on, 12
    catching floats, 16, 81, 85–87,
        159
    consistency, 16
    following charts, 9
    gauge, 9–12
    knitting with contrasting color
      in the left hand, 41
    knitting with main color in the
      right hand, 42
    long-tail cast on, 126–127
    marking the row, 15
    memorizing the pattern, 14
    Nordic, 33
    purling, 24, 119, 123–124, 186
    speed swatch, 11
    steam blocking, 17
    swatches and, 10–11
    tips for successful, 14–17
    tutorial for, 36–46
    tvinnarand edge, 130–131
    tvinnarand stitch, 128–129
    two-handed method, 19–20
    using beautiful yarn, 17
    using high-contrast yarn combinations, 15
    using knitting as a chart, 15
    using visual relationships, 14–15
    weaving in and out, 16, 38–39,
      44–45, 187
    working with ease, 12
    yarn dominance, 12–13
Continental knitting, 19–21
Continental purling, 24
contrasting color
    catching floats, 85–86

    holding in the left hand, 13, 16,
      41
    K2tog decrease, 184
    SSK decrease, 186
    weaving out, 44–45
cowls
    Sander Cowl, 35–46
    Setesdal Cowl, 91–94
crochet edges, 185

D

Dagna Hat, 95–99
dominant color, 12–13
double-pointed needles (DPNs),
    47, 183
duplicate stitch, 55, 183
duplicate stitch join, 183

E

ease, 12
embroidery
    duplicate stitch, 55
    French knot, 53–54
    lazy daisy stitch, 52
    Lovikka, 51–55
Emstad, Marit Gulsethbrua, 151
English knitting, 19, 21
Eva Jumper, 101–105

F

felting
    Lars Hat, 57, 60
    Olsen Slippers, 143, 146
    Stjerne Slippers, 121–122
    Swedish Lovikka Mittens, 47,
      49
Fleece and Harmony Selkirk Worsted, 169
floats
    catching, 16, 81
    catching contrasting color
      floats, 86
    catching main color floats, 87
    guidelines for catching, 85

staggering catching, 104, 159
    weaving in and out, 16
four-color knitting, 107, 113
Freja Hat, 75–79
French knot, 53–54, 183

G
garter stitch, 29–30
gauge, 9–12
Greta Pullover, 107–112

H
Harrisville Designs Highland
    Worsted, 121
Harrisville Designs Nightshades,
    95
Harrisville Designs WATERshed,
    122, 143
hats
    Dagna Hat, 95–99
    Freja Hat, 75–79
    Lars Hat, 57–60

I
Icelandic sweaters, 63, 73
Ingrid Fingerless Mitts, 169–172
intermediate 1 projects
    Eva Jumper, 101–105
    Greta Pullover, 107–112
    Linnea Pullover, 83–90
    Little Greta Pullover, 113–117
intermediate 2 projects
    Ingrid Fingerless Mitts, 169–172
    Kristiania Sweater, 173–181
    Little Haakon Sweater, 135–141
    Midsommar Pillow, 159–167
    Olsen Slippers, 143–150
    Selbu Mittens, 151–157
    Stjerne Slippers, 121–133

J
joining duplicate stitch, 183
joining in the round, 37, 183

K
K2tog decrease, 184
Kitchener stitch, 183–184
knitting techniques
    backward loop increase, 182

binding off, 182
buttonholes, 182
catching floats, 183
Continental, 19–21
with contrasting color in the
    left hand, 41
double-pointed needles
    (DPNs), 183
duplicate stitch, 183
duplicate stitch join, 183
English, 19, 21
French knot, 183
holding the yarn in the left
    hand, 22–23, 184
holding the yarn in the right
    hand, 25–26, 184
joining in the round, 37, 183
K2tog decrease, 184
Kitchener stitch, 183–184
lazy daisy stitch, 184
long-tail cast on, 184
with main color in the right
    hand, 42
making a crochet edge, 185
making a picot edge, 185
mattress stitch, 185
picking, 21
picking up stitches, 186
purl with two colors, 186
purling in the left hand, 24
purling in the right hand, 27
reading a chart, 186
running backstitch, 186
SL1-K2tog-psso decrease, 186
splicing yarn, 186
SSK decrease, 186
three-needle bind off, 187
throwing, 21
tvinnarand stitch, 187
two colors, left and right to-
    gether, 184
two-color long-tail cast on, 187
two-handed, 19–21, 23, 26
weaving a new color in, 38–39,
    187
weaving a new color out, 187
weaving out contrasting color,
    44–45

Kors og Kringle (Cross and Cook-
    ie) patterns, 35, 79, 91
Kristiania Sweater, 173–181

L
Lars Hat, 57–60
Latvian braid, 119, 128
lazy daisy stitch, 52, 184
Linnea Pullover, 83–90
Little Greta Pullover, 113–117
Little Haakon Sweater, 135–141
Liv Mitts, 29–30
long-tail cast on, 126–127, 184
Lovikka embroidery, 51

M
Magnus Pullover, 63–67
Maja Pullover, 69–74
mattress stitch, 185
Midsommar Pillow, 159–167
mittens and mitts
    Ingrid Fingerless Mitts, 169–172
    Liv Mitts, 29–30
    Selbu Mittens, 151–157
    Swedish Lovikka Mittens, 47–55

N
needle size
    gauge and, 9–11
    keeping watch on, 12
    swatches and, 10–11
Norwegian sweaters, 73
Norwegian Wool, 121, 151

O
Olsen, Arthur, 143
Olsen Slippers, 143–150
Ovis 21 Ultimate Merino Wool, 91

P
picking, 21
picking up stitches, 186
picot edges, 185
Pillow, Midsommar, 159–167
Plötulopi wool, 47
Prince Edward Island 2-ply Wool,
    169
purling
    colorwork and, 24, 119, 186

Continental, 24
  holding the yarn in the left
    hand, 24, 124
  holding the yarn in the right
    hand, 27, 123
  two-handed, 24

R
Rauma Finullgarn, 151
Rauma Strikkegarn, 121
Rauma Tumi, 79
ribbing, 36
rosemåling, 83
running backstitch, 186

S
Sander Cowl, 35–46
Scottish Lambswool, 107, 113, 135,
    159
seamless joins, 36–37
Selbu Mittens, 151–157
Selbu Star, 14
Setesdal Cowl, 91–94
SL1-K2tog-psso decrease, 186
slippers
  Olsen Slippers, 144–150
  Stjerne Slippers, 121–133
Soft Donegal wool, 57
speed swatch, 11
splicing yarn, 186
SSK decrease, 186
star motifs, 121, 143
steam blocking, 17
Stjerne Slippers, 121–133
Studio Donegal, 57
swatches, 10–11
sweaters
  Eva Jumper, 101–105
  Greta Pullover, 107–112
  Icelandic, 63, 73
  Kristiania Sweater, 173–181
  Linnea Pullover, 83–90
  Little Greta Pullover, 113–117
  Little Haakon Sweater, 135–141
  Magnus Pullover, 63–67
  Maja Pullover, 69–74
  Norwegian, 73
Swedish Lovikka Mittens, 47–55

T
three-color colorwork
  purling with two colors in the
    left hand, 24
  yarn dominance and, 13
three-needle bind off, 187
throwing, 21
tutorials
  backward loop increase, 182
  catching contrasting color
    floats, 86
  catching main color floats, 87
  contrasting color in the left
    hand, 41
  duplicate stitch, 55
  French knot, 53–54
  holding yard in the left hand,
    22
  holding yarn in the right hand,
    25
  joining in the round, 37
  knitting with yarn in the left
    hand, 23
  knitting with yarn in the right
    hand, 26
  Kors og Kringle (Cross and
    Cookie) pattern, 41–42
  lazy daisy stitch, 52
  main color in the right hand,
    42
  mattress stitch, 185
  purling in colorwork with left
    hand, 124
  purling in colorwork with right
    hand, 123
  purling with yarn in the left
    hand, 24
  purling with yarn in the right
    hand, 27
  two-color long-tail cast on,
    126–127
  weaving in a new color, 38–39
  weaving out contrasting color,
    44–45
  working a tvinnarand edge,
    130–131
tvinnarand stitch
  Latvian braid and, 119, 187

Midsommar Pillow, 161, 163
  Selbu Mittens, 151, 153
  Stjerne Slippers, 128–129, 132
  tutorial for, 130–131
two-color long-tail cast on, 187

V
Virgin Wool, 121–122, 143

W
weaving in a new color, 38–39
Woolfolk Får, 29
Woolfolk Tov-DK, 91

Y
yarn
  dominance in, 12–13
  holding in the left hand, 22
  holding in the left hand to knit,
    23, 184
  holding in the left hand to purl,
    24
  holding in the right hand, 25
  holding in the right hand to
    knit, 26, 184
  holding in the right hand to
    purl, 27
  splicing, 186
  using high-contrast combina-
    tions, 15

Z
Zimmermann, Elizabeth, 20